Christel Fiore

Child of War

By Christel Fiore

Copyright © 2006 by Christel Fiore

ISBN 0-7414-3143-2

Illustration by Christina Siravo

Published by:

PUBLISHING.COM

1094 New DeHaven Street, Suite 100
West Conshohocken, PA 19428-2713
Info@buybooksontheweb.com
www.buybooksontheweb.com
Toll-free (877) BUY BOOK
Local Phone (610) 941-9999
Fax (610) 941-9959

Printed in the United States of America
Printed on Recycled Paper
Published April 2006

Christel   Ulla

Gut Kamerat

This book is dedicated in loving memory
to my sister Ursula,
and to all children suffering in war.

Child of War

Countless movies and stories have been written by the victors of World War II, but few have been told by the losers of that conflict. I felt it might be interesting to hear from the other side, without accusation; just an account and a glimpse of average people caught up in events beyond their control.

I was five years old in 1938, living in Berlin, Germany, with my parents, my older sister Ulla, and our black and white male cat 'Schnucki', that Mutti had put in the baby carriage with me when he was just a tiny kitten. Schnucki played an important part in my life, since we grew up together and I could tell him all my troubles and deep thoughts when the lights went out for the night. We lived in a small apartment in a large building that housed quite a few families. My mother was the caretaker of the building, and Papa was an Electrician and plumber, earning an average family income. We had to help Mutti with the chores to keep the building clean and orderly. Our tree-lined street was pretty, with all necessary stores nestled neatly at the street level of the houses. A bakery, soap store, library, milk store, and right around the corner a most fascinating store that sold various types of toasted coffee beans, cookies, candies, chocolates and other heavenly, aroma-spreading goodies. Next to that store was an ice-cream parlor, which induced us to perform our chores with speed in order to reap the reward of a delicious tasty 10-pfennig ice cream cone.

Mutti had the habit of making us forego the reward by marching us into the neighborhood bank and opening a savings account for us. Unfortunately all monetary gifts went that hateful route also. We were lucky to have a sympathizer in Dad, who slipped us the necessary pennies to satisfy our sweet tooth more often than Mutti would have approved.

Our all-girl school was located several blocks away, strictly run by unmarried female teachers. The grownups referred to them as OLD MAIDS when they thought that we were not listening. They enjoyed total control, keeping us respectful, quiet, polite and productive. If necessary discipline was dispensed, it was unquestioned by our parents. Teachers, Police, and Elders had to be treated with utmost respect. The general rule was that children should be seen and not heard. So now that I have laid out the background, my story can begin.

It was a November night when I woke suddenly, with an uneasy feeling, to a strange energy-laden silence. My feet hit the cold linoleum floor as I left my warm bed in the dark to climb under my sister's covers for comfort, but her bed was empty. I rushed to my parent's room and entered without knocking, to find them standing silently at the window in the unlit room, watching the strange spectacle in the street. It was filled with many people walking like in an eerie parade, carrying lit torches and just shuffling along in absolute silence, with no beginning or end in sight. I tugged at Papa's sleeve, and he hoisted me up motioning to me not to make a sound. I whispered, "Papa, who are these people, and where are they going?" Papa hugged me before setting me on the floor with a slight pat on my buttocks. Pointing me the direction of the door, he told me to get back to bed. Ulla and I crawled under the covers, whispering back and forth about the strange events we had witnessed. I dropped off to sleep, looking forward to the next morning, because Mutti had promised to take me shopping for a new winter coat.

As the streetcar rambled past the display windows while I eagerly looked for the store, I noticed that on that day the windows were smashed or painted with a Star of David and 'Jude', written in big letters all over the vandalized storefronts. Mutti looked upset, reluctant to answer my questions in front of the other passengers, clenching my hand so tightly that it hurt. After leaving the tram, but as soon as we were out of earshot of the other passengers, she said that the people we had seen during the night with the torches had done all this. Again my 'WHY?' was left without answers.

My parent's social life was either the movies or the neighborhood Pub across the street for a nightcap and a bit of social interaction with friends and neighbors. Papa was good at playing the piano, and everyone joined in sing-alongs. We kids could join on occasion. I would brazenly belt out heavy love songs while standing on a chair, accompanied by my father, who encouraged me to sing loudly and breathe from my diaphragm. The renditions always earned me a bar of chocolate or a bottle of Coca Cola. Doctor Ravinowitch, our family friend and Physician, was my greatest fan; I was always welcome to visit his home, which was also his practice. He simply was there for us whenever we needed him. I thought of him as the most handsome man (beside my Papa, of course). His office had tufted leather doors and was very elegant, and his Terrier, Struppy, could lift the phone of the hook when it rang. Mutti took me there many times, because the good Doctor had decided to give me sunlamp treatments to enhance my sickly, pale appearance. He always said that if it was the last thing he would accomplish, it would be to put some color on me. He never succeeded though. Suddenly one evening he bid 'farewell' to my parents, and the next day he was gone, dog and all! He had fled Germany without telling anyone so that they would not get in trouble when questioned by the Gestapo. So slowly my life was changing, without my understanding or having answers to my 'Why's?' There were always rumors, but the adults would stop talking when kids entered the room. I got so tired of people brushing me aside, telling me to hush and stop asking these silly questions all the time. They would tell me that I wouldn't understand anyway!

My enrollment in the first grade was, as usual, celebrated as a special event, with the colorful large cardboard cone filled by well-wishers with candies and goodies for my entering into that new phase of life. I felt very special standing with all the other girls in the Aula (Assembly hall). The aula was filled with large flags with big swastikas around Hitler's picture. Well, we heard many speeches of our being the 'Future for the Fatherland', and long songs about being willing to die for Germany. Our arms were stuck out in the salute, and finally my arm got tired and my very special feeling went sour. So I rested my hand on the shoulder of the girl in front of me, only to get the evil eye from my mother. I jerked my arm back up as if having received an electric shock; however, my elated mood had taken a trip south. Then I got that dreaded speech and neck jerking from my mother saying, "Do not EVER, do you hear me? EVER draw attention to yourself again, and in front of all those people!"

So the tone was set. Don't ask questions and

don't draw attention to yourself. For some reason Ulla never encountered such problems, simply because she was three years older and wiser. She took me aside many times simply to make me shut my mouth. Not always with success, she would console me after a well-deserved spanking or long shunning by Mutti.

Then came the time when Papa received his draft order and went to the caserne to march, sing, and carry a rifle. He had done that already in the First World War, and now had the dubious honor of repeating the experience again, which for him was pure torture. Papa was neither political nor disciplined, neither punctual nor conforming. He was a man that believed in 'live and let live', a free spirit that drove my mother crazy at times. We girls adored him. But one day, he turned in his civilian ration card, received a military ID (Soldbuch), and marched out of our family life, leaving us in tears to face an uncertain future. It didn't take long for us to see that things were changing.

About that same time, my handsome young cousin died in Belgium. He was a Ltd in the cavalry, and I worshipped him. He would bring by many different fiancés, all of whom I hated. They, in turn, didn't like me either. Later, French prisoners appeared in our street, serving as furniture carriers, guarded by soldiers. We went to trade them a piece of bread for cute little animals they had made out of fuzzy pipe cleaners. One was a little black cat that I clutched in my hand as time and bombings went on, with absolute faith that no harm would come to me while I had it. I always had to reshape my 'cat' afterwards, because I had crushed him so badly when the bombs came whistling down on us. Later the prisoners were gone. I missed them and the worn out photos of their families, each with a story mostly told through hand gestures and a lot of guessing. To me they didn't look like the enemy; the whole thing just didn't make any sense.

Now and then coming home from school there would be a fire engine in our street and people standing around in silence. Then Mutti would tell us that someone "opened the gas" and died. The family was like our Doctor Ravinovitch, "Jewish," which had absolutely no meaning for me, but that was soon to change. The movies, the news, the posters plastered to the walls displaying hook-nosed, leering, ugly pictures of the Jewish 'traitors', who were dangerous to the Vaterland (Homeland). I knew of no one that looked like that, so I made no connection. Then came the time when the neighbors who we once knew so well could only go to the stores at night, like shadows in the dark;, they wore a curious yellow star on their clothing. Finally, when I would cheerfully greet them, they asked me not to do that anymore, leaving me confused, hurt, and asking why? How had I angered them? I didn't know that they just wanted to keep me out of trouble. After all, we were programmed later to understand what the adults already knew: 'do not be friendly with Jewish people; just forget having known them.' Mutti would just take me silently by her side. How could she explain these events to a seven-year-old child? I did not ask anymore from then on.

The first air raids by the RAF were a welcome diversion for us kids, since we sat for hours in the shelters listening to explosions here and there. This would give us late morning school days and plenty of playtime in the shelter. We would look up at the sky and say, "bombers' moon, late school tomorrow." Rain meant no alarm. We became quite the predictors. Well, that pattern didn't last long. The bombing left traces of the damage closer and closer to our part of the city. Soon, some girls in our school didn't show up anymore, and we would silently deduce that they were dead or somehow had left Berlin. Young girls joined the BDM (Band of German girls), looking all alike in their uniforms. We younger ones envied them. It was the same for the boys...uniforms and brainwashing. The teachers, wearing the party button proudly, did their job with the rest of us. "If you hear anyone, including your parents, talking about our Fuhrer in a negative fashion, you must report it immediately to a party member or authority. It is your duty as a German to defend your Vaterland against such traitors. "Your Vaterland and your Fuhrer are above everything and everybody," the message pronounced. No wonder the people stopped conversations whenever we were within earshot. And I repeated all that garbage! What did I know at my age? My mother didn't trust me anymore as far as she could spit, because all that crap flowed with great enthusiasm over my lips. My eagerness to get in to the uniform also pretty much convinced her that THEY had done quite a job on my immature brain. I recited data on Nazi history and was quite a saluter, with a hardy "HEIL HITLER" to boot.

We had one radio station with Hitler holding his very loud speeches, usually on Sundays. They were always preceded by Wagner's music. I never missed the occasion to listen, since we had to give an oral school report the next day. I was a 'gifted student', they said, 'great future!'

Hitler always came down Potsdamer Strasse, the main street next to ours, and I would be there to see him in his open Mercedes, while sitting between some tall SS soldier's wide-spread legs. I was a short, small kid, but always waved my little paper swastika flag that all children had. I was a steady on that corner with a 'reserved front spot,' so to speak. At one point I was lifted in to the Mercedes and got a handshake and a pet on my cheek, which I wiped off (to my mother's horror), and returned to my front spot between the legs of the storm trooper The SS guards were pretty much the same ones every time. They were ordered to form long human chains on that corner, presenting quite a sight in their black uniforms. There were also the SA in the brown uniforms, and a lot of policemen in green uniforms with high hats. I kind of got to know many of what I called 'my group', and when I announced that the next day would be my birthday, my perplexed mother opened the door to a few SS guards that presented me with flowers and a bar of chocolate. My existence somehow always revolved around uniformed men. (It seemed predestined.)

So life went on with occasional mail from Papa, who was a corporal and motorcycle messenger in France. He occasionally sent a box with goodies, like hard candies, French chocolates, cigarettes, and unroasted coffee beans for Mutti. That prompted quite a production of roasting the beans in the frying pan with the doors open, drawing half the neighborhood woman to our door to sniff that tantalizing aroma. The roasting usually culminated in a big Kafeeklatch (coffee party). Friends and neighbors eagerly sipped the brewed, bitter stuff. I was always puzzled by the obvious joy they got out of it. By then, there were only woman present, since most men went to war. Only a few super studs remained to keep the wives in a constant state of pregnancy, like brute mares. The remarkable birthrate in such a family was rewarded with a Mother cross on the entrance door, and HE had a pin next to his swastika on the lapel, plus extra rations to keep up his strength! That was his contribution to the homeland. Oh the stories the woman told at these gatherings over coffee. Mutti always cleared me out to go and play because, she explained, I had big ears and couldn't keep my mouth shut. However I managed to hear bits and pieces trying to figure out this 'baby' thing.

A bit later came the big change. One day when we came home from school, Mutti was busy packing suitcases, two of them to be precise. Most children had been ordered out of Berlin. Only real little ones, the toddlers and infants, went with their moms. The bigger ones, like Ulla and me, had to leave alone. Mutti was filling them according to a list, six each of underwear and stockings with name sewn in to the clothing, and so on. She was busy and stone faced, not letting us see her despair, and not being too clear on details. Finally we got a cardboard ID card around our necks from the Red Cross, and off to the train station we went, with hundreds of children all in the same boat. All were bewildered, frightened and pretty unwilling to leave. Mutti was biting back her tears as she lined us up with the other kids to board the train. Ulla was ten, and I had just turned seven. We had some sandwiches packed in a little black cotton sac that was hung around our neck, not unlike the feedbag on a horse. A nurse herded us on to train cubicles, their windows all boarded up except for a small square in the middle to peek out of. After all, there was a black out in effect. We bid a tearful good by, fighting for a place to get a last glimpse of the mothers standing on the platform, watching their children start a journey to an unknown place, with total strangers to care for them. My learned Nazi enthusiasm had now waned. All the events became uncomfortable and emotionally draining. Simply said, I was already becoming homesick and wanted my mother and my cat. To hell with all the promised glory awaiting us under the future 'German Reich..'

The swirling snowflakes performed a silent dance in the dim light of the slowly swinging metal lamp that sent a meager beam over the open snow-covered platform of the train station.

The late night had the stillness that only a heavy snowfall could bring. The silence was periodically interrupted by the puffing sounds of the locomotive taking on coal for the journey that still lay ahead. The warmly dressed sleepy station attendant carried his lit oil lamp carefully away from his moving legs, cursing the night duty under his breath. He glanced briefly at the children's faces that were pressed against the tiny squares of glass in the train cubicles. By now he was used to seeing the overloaded trains roll weekly through this station, filled with children from the big cities seeking refuge from the bombings, away from their mothers and homes. The children had been awakened by the jarring and stopping of the train. They had not enjoyed a sound sleep in their sitting position. Each time they tried to shift to be more comfortable, little shoves and nudges were exchanged, the way children do when they feel imposed upon. These kids had long passed their limit of tolerance and were now openly cranky. However, the nagging thirst and the imminent need to use the toilet was not enough reason to abandon one's seat, for fear that it would be taken by someone else. The discomfort for all was heightened by the shifting and hopping motions, accompanied by a constant crossing and uncrossing of legs trying to subdue the urge to urinate. Those unsuccessful ones with weaker bladders became painfully aware when they had lost the battle; with the warm relief came the awful smell throughout the compartment, making their accident so embarrassingly obvious. That in turn brought on loud protests and finger pointing, accompanied by cruel remarks that only children are capable of. Tears started to flow down shamed faces, and mothers' arms were sadly missed.

Without warning, the door to the compartment was thrown open, and a cold blast of air entered, along with the attending Red Cross nurse. She was annoyed at these kids for bothering her again and again, forcing her to leave her comfortable warm seat to settle one argument or another. She was tired of attending to these 'brat trains', and wished she were taking care of some wounded soldiers in a convalescent hospital somewhere, preferably in Bavaria. She had signed up to be with the heroes of the war, and this is what she got! –She was assigned a train full of sniveling, cranky kids, belonging to common people of no importance. Armed with a flashlight that she pointed at the children's squinting faces, she would bellow, "What's going on in here, for crying out loud?" She sniffed the air and screwed her nondescript face in to a grimace. "Aha! someone tinkled, thank you so much. Very considerate to the rest of us who have the pleasure of smelling that!" she snarled. She was letting the beam of light wander mercilessly from face to face. The children shrank in their seats, as if the beam had smacked them. They had fear in their eyes and wished that they were back in Berlin, even with the sirens going off at night and running to the air raid shelters. The nurse waved her ringless fat hands at the children that were asking for some water. She stuck the flashlight under her chin and produced a small bottle out of her coat pocket. With the other hand she fished out some sugar cubes. She popped the cork of the little bottle with her mouth and began putting some strong-smelling drops on the cubes, counting silently to ten and handing the cubes to each child. They eagerly popped this sweet treat in to their mouths, but right away experienced the slightly burning sensation of the drops. The train jolted and stopped as if in a hopeless attempt to leave this deserted station, and slowly moved forward, picking up speed and leaving the swinging light bulb behind waving a forlorn farewell.

The nurse slid the door shut, leaving the whiny, sleepy kids behind, knowing that soon the drops would take effect and sleep would overcome them. She went to her own compartment to get some shuteye, leaving the bothersome brood behind, and liking her job less by the second. She didn't even try to get a grip on herself and show some sort of compassion. What for? She was in charge and not interested in impressing anybody, least of all these mothers pleading to "Please take care of my little girls." Sure lady, just yours, no sweat. Only if necessary would she look at the cardboard dangling around the neck of a kid to get some information for whoever wanted to know. She certainly did not do anymore than absolutely necessary. Just a few hours more and this lot will be gone. Sometimes it seems as if the future foster parents take forever to select the children, she mused. She took a last long drag on her cigarette, opening the window slightly to flick out the still glowing butt. Some snowflakes hit her face, and she quickly slammed the window shut. She'll have to get out into that white stuff when they reach their destination, Sudetengau. She thought that maybe the snow would stop falling by then, and she closed her eyes, drifting into a light slumber.

The wind was blowing the snowflakes in all directions and it looked like a ballroom of happy dancers going around and turning to some waltz music that Ulla could not hear. She watched and almost swayed with the merriment that she observed through that little spot in the window. Her little sister tugging at her arm jolted her out of that happy feeling, and she heard the same question that she had been hearing so many times, "When we get back to Berlin, will Mutti be alive?" Although she was full of fear and doubt about the uncertain future, she replied, "Of course, Christel, she'll be fine." She could have used some assurances herself, but she had to take care of her younger sibling and be as convincing as possible. She loved her little sister dearly, but felt the role of the big girl weighing heavily on her shoulders. She was a mature ten-year-old, but even she could not hold back the tears, all the while hoping that her sister would not notice. Soon the tranquilizing drops took effect. Her eyes got heavy and she dozed off, involuntarily rocking back and forth with the rhythmic movement of the train.

They woke with a start and looked around in confusion. What happened? Where were they? There was a momentary shoving match, since everybody wanted to look out the window at the same time. Elbows and legs were used indiscriminately and all the penned-up frustrations of this miserable trip broke loose. Only the door opening and the ever so dis-gusted nurse, sucking the air in sharply, brought order in to the compartment. God! How they hated to have to listen to her endless stream of reprimands. But listen they did. She carried on about how German children should act, so that the Fatherland can be proud of them; how they are superior; and how Herr Hitler is looking out for their safety and wellbeing. She just didn't run out of words, and little foamy spit bubbles formed in the corners of her mouth. She was trained well.

Whistles were blowing and loud voices shouted orders as the doors were thrown open with a loud bang. The children huddled in their seats and no one wanted to be the first to venture out of the safety of the smelly cabin. They feared what was out there in the dark. The station looked the same as the last one they had stopped at. The open platform was full of snow, and there was a swinging light bulb that barely penetrated the windblown flakes. People stood huddled together, exchanging few words. They watched the children jumping reluctantly into the knee-high snowdrifts, sometimes landing on their knees or bottoms. No one laughed or bothered to wipe off the snow. The children just stared at the strangers and the approaching officials. Men in dark clothing and woman dressed like nurses with long capes. All the children were arranged two by two in a long line, the way they were taught all their lives (very important for Germans to form lines.) Ulla squeezed her sister's hand to reassure her, while everybody was herded in to a waiting room that was equally cold as outside, only minus the wind and snow. The light wasn't any better and the large empty room was dank and smelly. The strangers shuffled in also. There were few men amongst them. The woman wore kerchiefs in a babushka fashion, almost covering their foreheads completely. It was hard to see their faces, even when they came up close to pick out the child that they wanted. "I'll take this one," said a voice with a bit of an accent, grabbing Christel's hand. That's when Ulla hung on to her sister, thinking that she would never see her again. The girls were crying and fighting not to be separated. The nurse checked the cards on them and asked nonchalantly, "Do you want both? They are sisters." A redheaded lady in a fashionable coat with the swastika pin on her fur collar stepped forward and said, "I'll take the bigger one; this way they can live near each other." The nurse treated her in a doggish, subservient manner; she could not do enough for this woman, who seemed to be used to people kowtowing in her presence. So papers got signed, and they stepped outside in to an unknown country and life.

The tall woman was holding the small hand securely in hers while they walked laboriously through the snowdrifts toward the home that was looming in the foreground. Looking down, she realized that she had no clue what this child looked like, since all the events had taken place in the dark, and in great haste.

All the children were distraught, and the only reason why she picked this one was because she noticed two girls standing off to the side holding on to each other trying not to be noticed at all. She was now sorry not to have taken the two sisters, but comforted herself in knowing that Frau Wagner would make sure that the two would spend lots of time together in either house. The silent crying and occasional shudder of the child tugged at her heart, and again she was facing the misgivings of this war that brought nothing but misery and heartbreak to the innocent all over the world.

The long building suddenly appeared very clearly with a warm light shining on the glistening snow as if extending a welcome to the young stranger from a far away place. They entered through two huge wooden portals that led into a big cool hallway with a vaulted ceiling. To the left stood a double-doored cabinet with a shiny earthen pot on top. Next to it was a large round loaf of bread that the woman stuck under her arm before leading the child into the warm kitchen, which also offered all the comforts of a living room. The bay window was dressed with crisp white curtains, and the nook was furnished with a corner bench, topped with soft cushions to insure comfortable sitting at the table. It all looked very inviting, yet unappreciated by the newcomer.

Frau Kalni knew too well that for this night there was little to do. She warmed some milk, cut a slice of the enormous loaf of bread, buttered it, and noted with relief that nature in its glorious perfection did not disappoint her. The child managed to wolf down the bread and milk, however not stopping the flow of tears. Oh well, Christel thought, while undressing and sticking her hands in to the warm soapy water to wash that lousy trip off her body. Tomorrow will be better, she told herself. She reached into the suitcase that her mother had so lovingly filled and neatly arranged, not wanting to disturb anything, afraid that this very act would erase the last contact with her Mom. Frau Kalni helped without being intrusive; guiding her gently to what once was her daughter's room. Christel walked sleepily into the room, which smelled of fresh ripe apples, and slipped gratefully into a fluffy featherbed, drifting off to an exhausted sleep.

The door closed with an ever so slight click, just enough to wake me out of a sound dreamless sleep. I stretched under the warm featherbed cover and focused on my very attractive surroundings, inhaling the apple aroma that wafted through the room like an ever so pleasant cloud. I found myself in a room that was obviously decorated by loving hands for a very lucky girl. I thought that this was better than my room at home, and immediately felt a pang of guilt, feeling somewhat the traitor for the sense of pleasure these surroundings gave me. The events of the previous days crept in to my now wide-awake mind of the trip, the tall lady with her firm hand holding on to me, and my sister letting go of me. My suitcase was sitting empty on a chair, a clear reminder that I will be staying for a while. Somehow I resigned myself to that fact and concentrated on the hunger that drove me out of my bed into the very cozy inviting kitchen. What is it with me, I wondered? Am I supposed to be accepting these events simply by the need to be taken care of? Does that mean that I don't love Ulla and Mutti the way I should? Or was it that deep down, I knew that everything will be all right and things will be fine with my foster Mom taking care of me. No sirens, good food, toys and lots of visits with Ulla next door would be fine indeed.

The next seven weeks were spent with Christmas preparations: baking, handicrafts, and of course listening to the one radio station that kept us informed on the bombing raids over Germany. They also reported on the Blitz attacks over London. It made me think of those children living with the war like we were. Not Brits, just kids. The doubt and fear for those we left behind was constant. Was Mutti safe? Was our building still standing, or did she have to run to the neighborhood church where all the other bombed out people went? Would we know; would they tell us if she got killed?

Then came more news. I was up to my elbows in kneading cookie dough, without listening to the instructions as usual. There was a mess of flour all over the floor, on my face and pretty much throughout the nook. Tante Kalni did not mind or reproach me at all. Mutti would have blown a fuse to be sure. The letter in Tante Kalni's hand looked official, and she read it out loud. "All children that came with the last group will have to report one week before Christmas for their return to Berlin," she said. I was beside myself, jumping around with unbridled joy. I didn't even notice Tante Kalni swallowing her tears in dismay. No, just like an ungrateful spoiled brat, I acted as if I had been released out of a life sentence in a Siberian Gulag. This exuberance must have been painful to the woman who had given me so much, but she understood. When I left I did not realize what a wonderful person she was, nor did I know that our paths would cross again.

From that moment, nothing went fast enough. My eagerness to get back home was, to say the least, the ultimate example of ingratitude. I wouldn't shut up for one minute, no matter how Ulla tried to give me the signal, motioning to Tante Kalni's obvious distress. She carefully packed my FEED SACK with goodies, while I went on and on. In the morning the sky was heavy and grey, and we rose at dawn to beat the pending snowfall.

Our collection point was the bleak waiting room at the train station, the same as the night of our arrival. Only now we all stood there well-fed, rested, and indulged, with absolutely no worry about the long journey home. After receiving our cardboard ID, a hasty farewell, and a push and shove, we were back on the train--off to Berlin with a different nurse on board. It looked like everything would be just fine. We even started to sing. Occasionally the train stopped with a jolt as if it had gotten a surprise, and a long troop train would pass with soldiers waving and shouting greetings. We waved back and then watched the tanks and long artillery guns on flatcars swooshing by, ready for battle somewhere. The trip home seemed less stressful, since we could use the bathroom. However, we could not drink the water. That's when the magic drops came into play again, sending us in to la-la land, and leaving the nurse to her news journal with the weekly continuation of a love story.

I was watching the little houses whizzing by, some with lights on and people inside going about their daily routines. It was nice snooping on them without their knowledge. Then I drifted off with the rhythm of the train, my head tapping lightly on the window. We arrived at a train station that had been partially demolished by a recent air raid, bringing the war quickly back to our minds. The mothers, wearing the typical turban for those times, looked tired and anxious. It was quite obvious that they had not had a good time during our absence. Yet everyone got caught up in the happy reunion, a sentiment that held no cares or worries for me. I was happy to be back in Berlin. Little did I know that those happy moments would soon come to an end.

Shortly after our return, we became aware of a few changes. First of all, a couple of houses around the corner were missing, as if some crazed dentist had extracted a few teeth randomly here and there. The intact bricks were stacked in a neat fashion around the rubble of the ruins to give the impression of a low brick wall. Stuck to it were pieces of paper fluttering in the wind to give relatives and friends an idea where to find the former occupants of the building that once was their home. It felt strange to see the changes. Children inherently resent that. I certainly was on the top of that list. I also realized that no one can do anything about it and I would just have to hold still and deal with it.

The women were now openly referring to Feld-marshal Goering as "Herr Meier," since he had so boisterously announced, "If one bomb falls on Berlin, My name is Meier,"(A very common name like Smith.)

Going to bed in our underwear and stockings became a nightly affair, as were the bombing raids and runs to the shelter. Schnucki sat every night on the fence post of our very small front yard that displayed Mutti's petunias and a large chestnut tree. Without fail, my four legged "brother" would enter through his cat door and wake Mutti minutes before the alarm went off. We were always amazed at his uncanny hearing ability. Eventually, there came the time when I would hear the sirens in my dreams, only to have Mutti pull me up in bed with the result of me barfing all over her. Clearly she had to change her method of waking me! It also became clear to us that Schnucki could only handle the raids staged on clear nights with a full Moon. He also took to scurrying into our tile oven for cover, since pets could not come to the bomb shelter. After the air raids, many valiant people staged animal rescues out of blazing buildings, after the all clear signal had been given.

Daily life had changed drastically. All school-children were instructed to help the 'CAUSE.' So we had to go from house to house ringing bells to collect rags, tin, paper, bones, bomb shrapnel, and iron - in short, all sorts of garbage. The collecting was not all. In addition, we had to sort and bundle it. I can't describe the vocabulary that we heard after dumping this incredible stinky dirty bounty on Mutti's floor, getting it ready for the sorting. Then we had to bring it with us to school (whenever that was) and get it registered in our little Nazi handbook. The highest collector got a swastika pin in front of the full assembly. Well, Mutti put up with that crap as long as she had to, till the day came when Ulla and I broke out in a nasty red rash between our fingers. It eventually had crept over our hands, slowly moving across our whole body. The oozing and itching drove us absolutely nuts. The only treatment available was a yellow stinky sulfa solution that Mutti poured all over us while we stood butt naked on paper. The rest of the people treated us like lepers. Our hands were bandaged; we stunk, with the result of no school attendance. When that bout was over, Mutti decided that our contribution to the cause has reached its limits, and our garbage collection days came to a sudden end.

As it turned out, Fraulein Goethe, Ulla's teacher, had a problem with that unpatriotic decision. So in full assembly, she dared to point out my sister as a shameful example of a German girl that failed to support the Fatherland in its war effort. Ulla and I left the school shamed, like Adam and Eve banished from Paradise, shoulders hunched forward and heads down, we arrived home and gave a tearful account to our mother. Mutti had one untamable lock of hair that would rise under its own power standing straight up when she became angry. It was similar to a rooster's comb when aroused. Sure enough, we watched that lock of hair come up. She lit a cigarette and after taking some deep puffs, announced that she will pay that Fraulein Goethe a visit in class the next day.

Now let me tell you that we did not consider this visit as good. Mothers coming to school were always an iffy situation. What will she wear? How will she look? What will she say and what will the other girls think of my mother? All girls had the same phobia.

The next morning Fraulein Goethe came, as usual, through our street. Her dark grey straight cut coat buttoned to the top of her skinny neck. A little black felt hat with small rim as not to hide her hawkish thin face, plus a tightly wrapped bun peeking out over the coat's collar. She wore black shoes, with sensible heels, tightly laced. A black purse was held in one hand, and a black bulging business bag in the other. She walked erect and unblinking, all set to do her God-given duty. She was the perfect picture of the old maid. My mother's eyes narrowed watching this likeness of a scarecrow marching by, but not a word was uttered. Oh God, this will be a day to remember, we thought, as we made our way to school with Mutti telling us that she will be there LATER!

I listened to every sound in the hallway waiting for the dreadful moment of Mutti's entrance. Then I heard the sound of the front door slamming shut like a big GONG, as if to announce the beginning of the games. I heard the click, clicking of the high heels. So far so good, I thought. Then there was the knock and the opening of the door to Ulla's classroom. There was an angry murmur, followed by a bang on the wall. From what Ulla and everyone else said afterwards, Mutti had nailed the flabbergasted stick person to the wall and gave her the DON'T YOU EVER DO THAT TO MY DAUGHTER AGAIN!! With that Mutti left, and neither Ulla nor I was ever berated again. Fraulein Goethe used a different street from then on!

The day came all too soon that the suitcases lay open again with Mutti packing our listed mandatory clothing neatly into them. This time, she said, we are off to East Prussia, again without her, and again into unknown territory. Yes, we were almost two years older now since the last evacuation out of Berlin, but still unwilling to go. Papa had come on leave once for ten days and told us to always listen to Mutti no matter what. Then he left again, having spent little time with us because he and Mutti had diverted us to the movies or to go out and play. Obviously Ulla knew why, but chose not to share her knowledge with me. She did keep me out of the apartment with all kinds of tricks for lengthy times. My parents were always very happy and jovial when we returned, but evasive, and when I inquired as to how they had spent the time alone, Mutti would get downright nasty with her answers, while Papa would smile and wink at Ulla. She was always his favorite.

I resented Mutti's hoarding Papa all the time and would torture her with all kinds of stupid questions to the point of her throwing me out of the room, Ulla in tow ready to console my dramatic outburst of tears.

The departure date came swiftly; it was like a

replay of the previous journey. On to the train, hasty farewells, and a trip to forget! Our arrival in East Prussia was a definite downer. The train screeched toward the station past abandoned freight cars, rubbish-strewn tracks, and desolate platforms with disinterested station attendants glancing up at our train laboring by. Everything looked grey and hopeless. The city of Koenigsberg was covered in a grey fog, while a light drizzle misted this entire miserable scene. Now they have done it, I thought. They have sent us to a hellhole of no return. Even Ulla didn't have the strength to reassure me, nor did anyone else look optimistic, except of course the ever confident accompanying nurses that would not have to remain there with our doomed lot.

Then came the next shock. From the train, we were loaded on to various wooden horse carts, crusted with cow dung and remnants of straw and hay bits, to begin a trip through a bleak countryside of mud, drizzle, dirt, and total despair. The farmer guiding the two horses turned around and flashed us a toothless grin, contorting his unshaven face in to a hideous expression that was meant to be reassuring, I guess. We looked at him in sheer horror, and he never turned around again. Our destination was a town of grayish mud huts sprinkled here and there, surrounded by grey muddy earth interrupted by occasional poppy fields. This was God's spot for growing potatoes, poppies, cabbage, and some sort of sweet potatoes used for animal feed. Pigs roamed freely near the huts, which sported a huge dung mountain right next to the outhouse, thus making it possible for all to be used together come fertilizing time. It was indeed practical, but enough to make us want to puke.

The toothless wonder motioned me into the hut, which was almost as stinky as the crap mountain outside. Ulla got transferred to another cart, and so here I stood in a low ceiling room with a round clay oven in the middle. On top of it were several cackling hens and a couple of strange looking slant eyed, short men that had a big P painted on the back of their shoddy jackets. (Later I was told that they were Russian prisoners in a trusted position to help with the farm.) Anyway, I stood there nailed to the wood floor, frozen in disbelief that this should be my shelter, for whatever duration of time.

I sat down on my suitcase, letting no one touch it or me. I refused water, food or anything else that was offered, and remained silently crying through the stinky night. They came at dawn--the Red Cross, the mayor of this sinkhole of a town, and my teacher. Kind hands unglued me from my perch of protest, and I was taken to the town hall to be reassigned to the black-smith of the town, who already had another girl with him named Ingrid, also from Berlin.

The ride in a rickety coach was short, and I kept staring at the deep grooves in the road in order not to look at the miserable landscape. The lady next to me squeezed me into a corner with her big behind, and reassured me that Ulla had found a nice home on an ESTATE (meaning lots of horses and cattle with farmhands, and a Manor house.) She almost spoke of the place in a hushed tone. "It's only two kilometers up the road, and you can go visit whenever you have time," she said while patting me reassuringly on my head. "Of course your sister, being a fairly strong girl, will have to help with the chores. But you can visit anyway and kind of talk while she works." Again I felt the pat pat on my head. I ducked away from the petting hand and wished she would leave me alone in my misery, because whatever she said made me feel even worse. Poor Ulla, a servant for some rich people!

When I finally climbed off the coach, it leaned sideways as if to spit me out, and I almost fell in to the muck that was everywhere. I thought I had never left the place I had been first. The same hut, tiny windows and doors, 'Mount Merde', with the outhouse, the pigs digging their noses into the mud while throwing me a lazy glance. And then there were the geese. The gander started running towards me with open wings, hissing sounds escaping his partially open beak. I had never seen a living goose, only the ones ready for roasting, but I knew that this was the "Avenger" for all the geese that I had eaten in my short life. I just knew he would hurt me.

I burst through the door and found myself face to face with my new foster parents. They got up from a dark colored couch with a framed print of a poppy field in red bloom. That was the only color in the room. Everything was dark or colorless. The two people were old, but looked at me kindly. They were as simple as the house they lived in. The living room was sparsely furnished and provided no comfort. The kitchen was filled with a loud buzzing sound stemming from huge black flies all over the whitewashed walls adorned with long sticky flycatchers, already full with no room to spare. The stove was huddled in a corner across from the water pump, which had a groove running straight out through a hole in to the shit pile outside. The one other piece of furniture was a long type of buffet that also served as a table – workspace, with pots and pans underneath behind four doors, and an oil lamp on top. No electricity, I concluded. Then in entered Ingrid, the other happy traveler. She was pale, dark haired, and eager to show me to our room off to the side of the 'salon..'

The beds consisted of wooden boards on the floor which provided sides for the straw filled mattresses, which were covered with rough linen sheets - not white, not beige. We both burst out laughing hysterically, while at the same time fighting back the urge to cry. What did we ever do to deserve this? City slickers in a cow patch.

The most disgusting part however was that we had bed partners, the mice, which constantly rustled around in our hay and straw mattresses. They also seemed quite comfortable in the flour and poppy seed sacks that leaned against the wall in that small storage room. The entire thing was unreal, as were the breakfast, lunch, and dinner. It was a constant race to get a morsel of food in to one's mouth before a fly dove in. So it was spoon or fork in mouth, then finger in dish to fish out the kamikaze flies. They came from the dung heap next to the open kitchen drain hole with stagnant water puddles next to it. To further our thrills, we faced a two kilometer. walk to school. That was if we didn't take the shortcut through a pasture filled with cows and long horned steers. Those beasts would barely glance at us while we climbed the fence, but once inside, they would chase us with thundering hooves to the other side and over the fence. This was the "1943 East Prussian Pamplona", so to speak.

After several weeks of the combined experiences and a lot of vomiting, my body protested by developing large festering boils and a pussy crust around my mouth. I was oozing and seeping, giving everybody the creeps. With bandages from torn sheets hanging off of me like a risen Mummy, we went off to Koenigsberg to the Red Cross. The nurse had all she could do to hang on to her breakfast while she urged me NOT TO TOUCH ANYTHING!

It wasn't long before my condition brought about orders sending Ulla and me back to Berlin. We found out after the war that the Russians had in the meantime overrun that region, and many children never returned. So my body rot worked out well for us.

I fit right in with the wounded soldiers on the Red Cross train taking us back, and although we had to change trains a couple of times, Ulla got us back to Berlin. Things had changed dramatically during our absence. The former trade school three houses down was now loaded with soldiers. The individual classrooms were filled with bunk beds, and long wooden tables with benches served the troops for all other needs. They got one hot meal served in their mess gear, cooked in the courtyard in a big, wheeled boiler pot (Gulasch canon.) It was fascinating to be around during those feedings, plus I found the food delicious. That environment sported the extra bonus of dirty drawings and filthy scribbling on the toilet stalls, which provided me with a full sex education, till Ulla caught me and that was that!

Our air raid shelter was underneath the six story solid brick building. It had big steel doors, with a vacuum lock that sealed all air out in case of a gas attack. There were large pipes running across the low ceilings, and the light bulbs were set in metal casings. It was dank down there and smelled of wet cement. Long benches sat along the walls and through the middle. People in the middle sat back to back. The air raids now came in rapid succession, making any form of normal living impossible. Electricity, water and gas services hardly existed. The public transportation was intermittent, and entire neighborhoods got reduced to smoking rubble. Many women dressed in black, mourning the loss of loved ones.

Young girls had been taken to places outside of Berlin and returned after many months, shadows of themselves, and barely speaking. We heard later about the breeding places, where young SS soldiers fathered babies. The mothers got sent back after delivery, minus the babies. The program was called 'Hitler's Children', who were to be raised by true blue Nazis. After all, these were pure Arian kids.

We learned to sit through the bombing raids with our fingers stuck in our ears and our mouths wide open, while the pressure from the explosions swooshed through the shelter, seemingly sucking all the air with them. They said that the bombs that we heard whistling wouldn't hit you. I always wondered about the ones that we didn't hear?

Outside, we amused ourselves watching various new people that moved into the neighborhood, since the authorities subdivided intact apartments for the air raid victims. So we wound up taking in people that had lived somewhere else. Our place was now two rooms smaller, two given to a single female with a dubious profession. Her name was Ilse. She had many male visitors who remained for short visits, and who always used the back entrance, thus escaping our curious eyes. Mutti had put our big wardrobe in front of the door that used to lead to those two rooms. However, we could still hear strange sounds coming from behind that closet, and wondered just what the hell was going on there.

With the new influx of people came the addition of a short fat guy in a brown SA uniform that puffed him up with authority, making up for the fact that he was not fit to be serving at the front. He scrutinized us all through his beady eyes, which were framed by dark rimmed glasses that gave him a sinister appearance. We watched him with amusement, waddling across the street in slippers to get his bread in the morning, his short arm clutching the newspaper. He was hardly a figure that would command our respect or admiration. He became, however, quite an obstacle in our already turbulent life. When the sirens went off, sometimes simultaneously with the first bombs whistling down on us, this queer gift to humanity would push woman and children out of the way to get his fat ass into the air raid shelter. People knew that he was potentially dangerous because his presence was justified by his mission: to report any rumblings of dissent to the authorities. In short he was the neighborhood Nazi watchdog. On one bombing occasion, he rushed through us on the crowded staircase, knocking people against the wall to plant himself on the wall bench. That enabled him to keep his eyes on everybody. This particular raid was very heavy, and seemed to have concentrated on our part of the city. We could hardly breathe and cowered under the bomb blasts, praying for relief. Some people threw themselves to the floor when the cement started to snow down on us, and the walls showed cracks opening in different parts.. So 'fat stuff' then took refuge on the middle bench, landing him back to back with my mother.

The old air raid warden whose job it was to go out into this hell and give a damage report to us came back covered in cement dust and soot, visibly distraught and hardly able to announce, "They have the Christmas trees set up on top of us!" That meant that our neighborhood was lit by flare bombs to make it a better target to hit. It was now our turn, and mothers embraced their children tightly, crying in fear.

The poor old man, at his advanced age, ventured out, driven by a sense of duty that was put on him to serve Germany. So here he was, going into hell and fire to return with the bad tidings of buildings gone or burning. People's belongings and homes were no more. After one of these announcements, Mutti wept, saying, "Oh, those poor people," and immediately the fat finger of that creep poked her in the back. As she turned, he looked her straight in the face and said, "This, my good woman, is the price we have to pay for having a TOTAL WAR. Heil Hitler!"

Mutti looked at him in disbelief, took a deep breath, but wisely said nothing. Shortly afterward, a bomb found, amongst others, the misfit's house. He threw his stubby arms into the air, wailing loudly that now he had lost everything! My mother poked her finger in to his back, and as he turned his tear-streaked face to her, she said, "That's the price we have to pay for having a TOTAL WAR and HEIL HITLER TO YOU!"

Even under those horrendous conditions and with all the fear that consumed me, I was able to feel that somehow in war, justice was quick to come, and it was my mother that had dished it out this time!

After the raid was over, we left the shelter to go into the fiery scene that was once our street. Big fireballs flew around us from the burning buildings across the street, and screams echoed from those that hadn't had time to make it into a shelter. The heat was unbearable; there was no escaping the reality of destruction. We ran through a shower of burning cinders, trying to find shelter while ducking pieces of burning roofs. Our building was standing, but burning at the top. The big heavy entrance portals leading to the apartments were gone; so were the windows and doors. Weeping, disoriented people stumbled and fell onto the broken glass in the street, trying to find what was once their home. My aunt was singing and waving her arms, her hair smoking and standing straight into the air. She had gone crazy in the shelter and was put away, never to be seen or heard from again.

We hardly had assessed our situation before the sirens went off again, and we ran back to the shelter. This time it was dark. There was no more electricity, leaving us to endure the brutal explosions by the flickering light of a candle. This time when we came out, water was spouting from holes in the street where the pumps had been. Rubble, trees, and some animals lay strewn in what was once a pretty place. Although it was morning, we had hardly any daylight because of the burning fires and smoke. We were told by loud-speaker cars to go a few blocks away to the Maggi factory to get food rations. Mutti grabbed a laundry basket that had landed in our front yard amongst all kinds of stuff. We followed the chain of people through the destroyed streets to the Maggi house. We entered down a steep ramp in to a very large, cool basement that had armed soldiers standing along the walls. Somehow I thought that now we were going to be shot, because they did not know what to do with all of us needy people. It seemed to me that this would be the next solution for us. After all, that stay in East Prussia was to me like a bad Omen, telling me that we were truly of no value.

Suddenly, two big panels behind the soldiers slid open revealing long tables laden with food and fruits that we had not seen in a long time. We had only gotten some such goodies on a special ration coupon for particular holidays. The Red Cross personnel instructed us to come forward when called in alpha-betically order. Our name started with a "G", so our wait was not too long. Mutti marched with the two of us to the designated table, signed the list, and pre-sented the laundry basket, which I hoped they would fill. No such luck. We got wrapped salami and liverwurst sandwiches for each, along with four apples, oranges, some cheese. We also got a handful of hard candies, bottled milk, and some canned fish. We earmarked the fish immediately for poor Schnucki, who had greeted us after the air raid barely able to croke a mew. Then we joined another line and received a metal dish of potato soup that we downed right then and there. After that Mutti did what she always did when she deemed it necessary; she gave her handkerchief a quick lick and wiped the remains of the onions from around my mouth. God, how I hated that kind of a face wash!

We went to what was left of our home. The bedding had jagged pieces of glass sticking out of it here and there, making it dangerous to sleep in or on. The air was thick with smoke and ashes flying through the holes that had been our windows. Mutti looked at what was at one time a neat little apartment, which she had kept comfortable for her family. Now there was no resemblance, and it was hard to imagine the many happy moments that we had enjoyed in those walls. She wiped a tear that ran down her soot-covered face, and decided to get us out of Berlin. With that announcement, the sirens wailed again, and we fled back to the shelter, leaving Schnucki in front of an open sardine can and a partially broken dish of milk.

This time the raid hit more or less another neighborhood, judging by the whistling of the bombs, which was every now and then interrupted by the tat-a-tat tat of the anti air flak, followed by a tremendous explosion that lifted us out of our seats. We found out later that some of the bombers were shot down over us by the air defense guns, at times crashing, bomb load and all. We could not form a clear thought just huddling by candlelight with those awful explosions rattling our brains. We knew that we had to get out and in to that disaster sooner or later, unless the building collapsed on top of us, and then what? It happened on the corner. People were frantically digging through the rubble to free the trapped families, sadly until the feeble knocking on the pipes stopped. Every woman and child had suffocated. When we finally left on foot, burnt bodies looking like charred wood had been arranged for possible identification. How could anyone tell who is who? They were once our neighbors, people that I knew. Mutti tried to shield our eyes, but we had to walk past the dead. And so it went for blocks, one after the other.

We finally got an underground train to take us out of the city to the suburbs, and after many maneuvers on different means of transportations, we reached my godmother's town which was intact and showed no sign of bombardments. We were so exhausted, too exhausted to wonder or even notice the strange hustle of activity of many German soldiers running back and forth. There was nothing that could have piqued our curiosity. Our eyes were swollen and too tired to take in or wonder about this strange activity.

Tante Agnes was standing in her yard when we arrived. We were looking tired, dirty, exhausted and yet overjoyed to have reached our destination. I immediately left my makeshift luggage in the middle of the street, yelling at Ulla over my shoulder to bring it with her. Never mind that she had her own stuff to carry. She patiently gathered up my load as usual, without complaint, having been exposed to my inconsiderateness for some time. It was Mutti that caught me by my collar, bringing me to a screeching halt in my trot. She gave me a solid smack in the head which made my hair and stars fly in front of my eyes. She spared me the verbal tirade that usually followed her dispensations of the quick and what I considered sneaky discipline. To her I was a hopeless case of an unbelievably selfish human being with a minimum of character. I guess she expected better from me under the circumstances. The hit jarred me, and when Ulla came, as always, to console me, I felt a sense of shame on top of a lingering smarting of the head.

We went straight to the yard to greet Tante Agnes, with Mutti apologizing profusely about our unannounced appearance. Meanwhile, Tante Agnes was poopooing Mutti's sentences with a genuine relief at seeing us alive and well. Tears of joy were streaming down her cheeks as she ushered us in to her apartment. The news reports with only one station were so limited, usually only announcing how many bombers had been shot down during the raids. Of course we had heard them come down, but didn't know how many.

Tante Agnes was always an uncomplicated, well-adjusted, and deeply caring individual with us, taking her job as godmother very seriously; plus she was once married to my father. They divorced after seven years because she could not have children. Papa in his infinite wisdom, made a trial run, to be on the right track so to speak. Ergo, Mutti was pregnant

43

when they married. Of course, one could also say that his free spirit had a good deal to do with that development, but however it played out, Ulla and I never knew about those events.

Be that as it may, everyone remained friends with Tante Agnes as our godmother, who always had an active part in our lives. During the peaceful times, our family outings took us on a weekend visit with her and her new husband, a publisher with a fully equipped office. While there, we could do no wrong. And the typewriters and papers piqued our imagination to play secretaries. The small town on the outskirts of Berlin, gave us lots of roaming space while the adults drank wine, smoked, and had themselves a party. We kids would show up for meals, only to run off again. The evenings were filled with piano playing, with Mutti always singing in a vibrato voice which I absolutely detested. IT was so bad, I would ask her all kinds of stupid questions to stop the "awful noise" she was making. No matter how I tried, she would either nod for yes, or shake her curly head for no, usually accompanied by a well-manicured finger waving back and forth.

When I became too much of a pain in the rear, she would grab me by my arm and expedite me out the door, never skipping a note in the process. In turn Ulla and I learned to ape her voice and motions to perfection. When caught during our exhibitions, we triggered rib roaring laughter; the punishment was severe but well worth it.

So now we were there as homeless refugees,

husbands and happy times now in the past. The war had not caused any visual damage. The services functioned, and the pleasure of getting water out of a faucet became a real luxury for us after having been without. We had fake coffee, fresh rolls, and while the woman smoked, the conversation went to the military hustle and bustle that we had witnessed on arrival. Wondering what that was all about, Ulla and I went by bike to take another look, only to be chased away by some armed soldiers standing guard. They let us know in clear language to get the hell out of there!!

I was pinched because I had always considered myself the little charmer that no one could resist. Well, not this time! We had eyed the big camouflage nets strung over the large area of frantic activity. Huge trucks were rolling in, guided by soldiers with sweat drops running down their faces, screaming commands over the roar of the trucks.

We popped back into the kitchen with all that we had seen and heard, setting off speculations and a smoking binge, both women disregarding the fact that cigarettes were rationed. Then Tante Agnes got the special cards out to see what's happening. That, by the way, became a ritual, kind of like a daily menu. The cards remained in sight on the kitchen table. It was the only deck she ever used, old and faded from having been handled over so many years. She was an expert in the reading of these cards. We had witnessed it often even as little kids. She was amazing at it, and many a woman would come to have her read for them in order to see if their husband, son or both are still amongst the living at the front; to predict the possibility of mail arriving, good or bad, in short all things that were close to peoples' hearts. From what I remember, Tante Agnes was never wrong with her readings, plus she never took money. She just had that special way about her, so different from Mutti's down to earth by the clock personality.

She deftly laid out the cards, and told Mutti that there were great changes coming to the town; there would be a bleak impact to our life, but we would survive. The place that we had escaped to seeking refuge from Berlin was going to be an area of dangerous events. In the next few days we discovered that in fact, we had jumped from the frying pan in to the fire.

The long fingers of the search lights wandered silently across the night sky, crossing each other at random points, then glided back and forth, silently standing guard over the heavenly frontier. The powerful beams above us had become a common sight while we were in Berlin; somehow we did not expect to see them here in that little suburb. Tante Agnes looked up, and whispered to Mutti, who nodded as she watched the beams go back and forth. She was, taking deep drags on her cigarette, ready to light a new one on the glowing stub. She was visibly nervous, and we had to go to bed with our clothes on.

During the night we heard the all too familiar humming of the approaching bomber squads flying over the town, and we jumped out of bed to watch them get caught in the merciless lights. Trapped like silver birds, slowly trying to escape into the elusive dark, but relentlessly staying on track to reach Berlin to unload the bombs that they carried in their bellies. We watched the German fighter planes engage the bombers, their munitions creating colorful streaks between the hunter and the hunted. It looked so beautiful, and we only ran for cover when we saw the first bomber go in to his deadly dive before crashing and exploding in the nearby woodland. We had hit the kitchen floor, covering our heads instinctively with our arms, however stupid that seemed afterwards. So it went on with intense explosions between the fighting planes, the premature discharge of the bombs from damaged bombers, and some ungodly big booms that we had never heard before. During all that we realized that we had no shelter to even protect us from flying glass or shrapnel. We crawled closer and closer together into a tight embrace, jolting with every explosion, listening to the windows shatter and watching kitchen utensils flying through the air.

Then came the silence. We just remained on the floor, and probably would have been there for the rest of the night had there not been a young air force lieutenant who broke the silence by asking if we had seen the first bomber come down, and maybe could we point him in that direction? He proudly announced that this was his first kill, and he would like to see it. He was handsome and in a proud sporting mood. As if this were all a big game.

Actually, we had seen that first bomber come

down before we hit the floor, and volunteered to take him to where we thought the plane crashed. He went slowly on his motorbike, while we followed him through the smoke of fires, shouting directions until we reached the spot that was already cordoned off and surrounded by people and soldiers.

It was a big plane, billowing smoke masking scorched bodies, partially visible hanging in the wreck. Mutti and Tante Agnes were ushering us away from the gruesome scene that they had for some reason not expected. For me it was too late. I had taken in all the details, and although the features of any of the crew were not distinguishable, I had seen the face of the enemy! Now it was not just noise and bombs coming to kill me, but there was a face and body attached to the killer. It turned in to a festering hatred and anger.

Later, Ulla and I went on an exploration mission back to the busy place from which we had gotten chased away, and surprise surprise, people had been creative. There were railroad tracks under the camouflage netting. The tracks made a huge circle from what we could spot, and on top of the tracks sat a huge canon ready to roll. It was like someone had set up a decoration under the Christmas tree for a giant, only instead of a train, this was a huge canon. They had given this small town a BIG BERTHA. We learned all too soon the consequences of the town's new addition. It didn't take a mental giant to figure out what the 'Uppers' had in mind, with this thing sitting there ready to blast at the approaching planes; as if the anti-aircraft flak had not been sufficient, and obviously not taken seriously enough by the allied bombers.

So the war had followed us here, and there was no place to hide from it. That was soon to change. The digging started with great fervor creating deep trenches in the forest and parks, covered by heavy boulders, sandbags and earth. We had to get down a steep dirt path and take our seat on boards along the makeshift walls, covered by long wooden flat boards to keep the sand at bay. The entrance and exit faced in opposite directions. It was like entering a grave by candlelight, with the musty dank smell of earth beckoning us in to its cool interior. The famous 'Splittergraben' (shrapnel grave) was the solution by the leadership to our predicament.

So there we huddled night after night, while Big Bertha turned into quite a dilemma for the enemy, since she was not a standing, but rather a moving target. The bombs fell kind of willy-nilly around her, damaging the tracks and hitting civilian targets. The tracks got quickly repaired, and so the games continued, while we again sat with our mouth wide open, fingers in the ears, hoping that the damned trench would not collapse and bury us all. When the sand started to drizzle down on us freed by the infernal blasts, we ran out taking our chances in the open air, clawing the earth and digging small indented spots like a dog creating a bed for itself.

In the middle of all this, Mutti felt that she had to get back in to Berlin to check on some of our family, and of course on Schnucki, who she had left in a neighbor's care. Who knew what had taken place there? We didn't get any news or mail. It was a gutsy undertaking into the unknown, with almost nonexistent transportation and unbelievable detours. Yet she went, and we swore never to imitate her singing again.

It was a wonderful day when she came back, especially with the cat, which was sitting in a laundry basket covered by a tied down sheet. Mutti had traveled through hell and high water to reunite him with us. We were thrilled to death, and could not thank her enough. Schnucki climbed out of his abode, stretched his legs, and finished a bowl of milk. We marveled at him as if he were one of the great wonders of the world.

The family had left notes, but Mutti could not maneuver around in Berlin because it was so heavily damaged. However, there was a letter waiting for her from Tante Kalni. It had been hand-carried by a soldier. In that letter she told Mutti to get out of Berlin with us kids and back to the Sudeten, where she has a room waiting for us. Boy, were we ready! In a short time, and with very little information as what train would go where and how long the trip would take, we kissed Tante Agnes and Schnucki good-bye, while Mutti promised her to come back 'after the kids are safe.'

We took off to catch somewhat of a train in somewhat of a train station, loaded with people that hardly had standing room on the platform. Everyone was in a foul mood, anticipating being first on the train. It was a brutal push and shove contest, not even giving consideration to the smallest of the children in their mothers' arms. We stood back so as not to be shoved on to the tracks, also using our elbows in defense, shoving back with all our might. The wave of people behind us pushed us on to the train, and we secured a seat in the over crowded compartment. Those who did not get on hung to the outside, clinging to door handles or any available protrusion. The locomotive was fired by coal, and the sparks attracted strafing from enemy fighter planes that accompanied the bombers. It was an exciting trip to say the least, and several people eventually fell off their perches, tumbling like big rag dolls to the ground.

We arrived in Prague in the middle of the second night of travel. Mutti handed the address to a makeshift taxi. As we arrived and entered the house, the welcome smell of a delicious meal beckoned us to come and find peace. There they were, the two women, not only drastically different in appearance but from different countries so to speak, bound together in the quest to survive this war and keep us, the children, safe. Just like women and mothers everywhere.

Tante Kalni had no idea where her son was or if he was still alive, but that did not make her indifferent to our plight and the danger that we had been in. I was so happy to see her again after the almost three years that had passed since I was in her care. She was overjoyed and fussed over us, filling our dishes with steaming stew, and slicing big slabs of bread-- urging us on to eat and enjoy. It didn't take much prodding after the trip without the needed food.

The apartment in Prague was not as cozy, but it was equipped with more modern conveniences than the house in Lichtenau where Ulla and I had been. However, that's where the 'room' awaited us. She apologized for the sparse furnishings awaiting us, explaining that it was in the back of her usual home, the front unfortunately taken over by some big shot party member.

The next day we were off to our new safe haven. The locomotive huffed and puffed through the peace-ful countryside slowly enough for us to marvel at the wonders of nature in its abundance and beauty. Hills, brooks and forests with birch trees seemed to stand at attention to greet us, the newcomers. And looking over the neat rows of farm plots and grazing cows, it was hard to reconcile the rubble and corpses that we had left behind with this picture-like landscape.

As we got closer and closer in to the familiar

surroundings, we deluged Mutti with stories of different experiences and memories that we had enjoyed here and there. We practically dragged her to the back of the house, nervously waiting for her to turn the key in the rusty lock so we could enter the tiny foyer that connected the room opposite with a toilet, which lacked every comfort.

The room was long enough for one bed and a couch to stand in a row with a table in front of them. On the wall was a small closet with a mirror in the front door that directly faced a stove and a metal wash stand on the opposite wall. A window next to the closet faced the train station, which was situated across a field of grass. Around the corner was a shed, well stocked with wood and kindling. Near the front door was a water pump with an ornate handle and a big bucket, just like Tante Kalni had said, very basic but functional. Certainly after bombed out Berlin, it was a definite improvement.

We were safe and knew that the adjustment would be easy. Our gratitude outweighed everything. As Mutti unpacked the personal things that she had crammed in to the suitcase, we were amazed as the room took on a more personal touch, and order took shape. When she started to talk school enrollment after a couple of days, our faces dropped, because that prospect did not appeal to us. Nevertheless, we got marched in to the small town square, with the school-house and mayor's official building, country store, and doctor's office all in a circle, and a fountain in the middle. Every building had a Nazi flag fluttering on its façade, crassly reminding us that there was a war on. The women were standing around in their dark clothing, with headscarves almost covering their eyebrows. They whispered to each other as we were approaching. They scrutinized this blond woman with her obvious city clothing, trying to figure out who and what we are.

The school consisted of one room with three rows of benches facing the blackboard, and of course the ever present flag. Yes, and then we came face to face with the booby price, the teacher, Herr Tauber! He had slammed the door of the school office so forcefully, that the echo reverberated through out the empty hallway. It must have been of great importance to him to make this noisy, macho entrance for effect, in order to compensate for his obvious physical shortcomings. He was definitely not the image of the German ideal that Hitler held so close to his heart. In fact, he could have easily passed as a relative of our Nazi watchdog that we left behind in Berlin. He was stocky and red faced, with short arms and legs - a bit gnomish. He stood in front of my mother, sucking the air through his yellowing teeth and exposing them with each breath he took. Lifting up and down on his feet, he exuded a form of impatience and superiority. His beady eyes scanned Mutti and us, while his hand repeatedly smoothed his slick, oily, ash brown hair with one careful motion. The suit matched his color-less appearance, while the round party button on the lapel let us know that he is in fact a Nazi person of importance not to be underestimated. What it came down to was that he was schoolmaster and principal all rolled in to one. Three classes wouldl attend at the same time for half-day sessions, including Saturdays. He was barking out the information as his face got redder, and the neck artery swelled right along with the throbbing vein in his temple. He was as short tempered and agitated as a newborn scorpion. Mutti gathered up all the necessary information and paper-work, while we looked abjectly at our future with that tyrant. We just could not win for losing!

Our first day of attendance went as expected. He pointed us out as 'THE BERLINERS' on every occasion he could summon. Needless to say, our classmates treated us as negatively and cynically as possible in order to please that piece of crap, for fear of becoming a victim themselves. Thank God Ulla and I had each other.

Again Mutti decided to return to Berlin to get her sewing machine and Schnucki. I must say now in retrospect that she had more gumption than many a person that crossed my path. Off she went, determined to get some sewing piecework with the machine. The room was small, but she had it all figured out, and the money was absolutely needed. We were left behind wondering if we would ever see her again, but thank God, return she did. We had Schnucki, and she had her Singer with the contract for piecework. It almost took artistic maneuvers to get around the room for anything. A needed dash to the toilet was as good as impossible with all the obstructions in the way. Though it was a relief when one would go to the toilet; then the other two could enjoy a bit of breathing space.

Soon Mutti was approached by a young widow who was left to tend to a small farm which was to produce the mandated food quota. She was a shy young woman who needed help, and she would be only too happy if Ulla could come and stay with her. She could have her own room and eat well, while also being of some company to the lonely woman. So all considered Ulla went voluntarily, although slowly Mutti and I found ourselves visiting frequently. Mutti was not one to sit under a cow to milk it, but I was game for this whole farm bit. That included harvest time, with all its hard work and great moments in nature, like fresh milk and eggs, and mashed potatoes with lumps of fried bacon in the evening. Ulla was happy, and I learned how to tend to newborn calves. Those gentle cows with their benevolent big eyes became my pets, and they followed me to and from the field with slow lumbering strides, licking my arm with the huge tongue when petted between the horns.

So life went on with a certain order. I learned to concentrate on the enjoyable parts and totally dismiss the unpleasantness of that miserable Tauber person. Meanwhile, Mutti had met another seamstress from Berlin, and the two of them got together whenever the need to relax arose. They would create billowing clouds, smoking and playing cards. Every now and then, there was a movie to go to at the train station collection point. That's where we got informed of the atrocities that our enemies had inflicted on the German populace when they got captured. We were petrified of the Russians, the Poles, the Czechs and so on. And we knew what the Americans could do from the air.

Weekends, and vacations had to be dedicated to collecting herbs and certain flowers for medicines. Also, ripping sheets into bandages and plucking threads to make stuffing for little cushions to stop bleeding wounds was a duty that no one shirked. After all, the troops needed everything. Knitting scarves, gloves, and socks, from recycled wool garments was another pastime. Our soldiers were freezing in the Russian winter doing their country's bidding, and we were there to support them.

Dresden got wiped out, Stalingrad fell, and a group of officers working with Hitler tried to blow him up. These are the news events that stuck in my mind, as well as the constant talk of the V3. The V1 and V2 had already created havoc over England. What was this promise of the super weapon? We never found out, because we became painfully aware of the constant and ever increasing flow of refugees on trains and country roads.

Yet, all along Herr Tauber became more irate, ignoring the developing events around us. His little stick came whistling down on our desks for whatever reason, and it seemed to me that he spent more and more time on glorifying OUR FUERER. We sang and recited Hitler data, afraid that this little harassed pig was going to do us in if given the chance. I had been barfing through the bombing raids, but I now outdid myself with insufferable migraine headaches, while everyone insisted that kids my age do not have a migraine--basta! I missed a lot of school, but got saved by my love for reading.

I did however watch the events unfolding with an ominous feeling that life was changing again. First came the trains rolling through the station with people hanging on to the outside wherever they could, even sitting on top of the roofs holding on for dear life, while the lucky ones that had gotten inside were squashed against the windows. Every so often, the train would slow down enough for the corpses to be thrown out, to remain next to the tracks like broken dolls in grotesque positions. Later, cattle cars full of livestock would stop and every capable person was summoned to grab a bucket to milk the cows that were screaming in pain with inflamed huge udders that needed to be emptied. Ulla was one of the valiant ones to climb on and get in between the crazed animals to help out. The dead and dying cattle got thrown out and left behind also. Some ambitious farmhand would bleed some of the poor beasts and slice chunks of meat out of them before they had a chance to be in a state of death.

So slowly the field of grass leading to the station turned in to a hastily dug graveyard/slaughterhouse combination. Looking down the dusty country road, the endless wagon trains had no beginning and no end. Exhausted cows with their hooves stretched out of shape exposed the bloody stumps from walking on the rough rocky roads, pulling the wagons while feeling the sting of the merciless whip on their strained backs to keep them moving. The wagons were laden with bedding, food stuffs, water barrels, and possessions that would eventually wind up in the ditches on either side of the road, along with the sick, dying people and animals. Though I was taking all that in, I never gave it a clear thought as to what all this will mean to us and our survival. The dust that glimmered in the bright sunlight made the wagons, the humans, and the beasts appear like they were moving through clouds, and even muffled out the sounds.

When Mutti called out for me to get immediately to the room, I obeyed, shut the door behind me, and made believe that nothing of what I had observed was real or of any consequence to our future. People had dragged a dead cow near to our building, leaving the bloated cut up body with an exposed form of an unborn calf for the unbelievable swarms of black flies, buzzing their song of death while depositing mountains of maggots on the decomposing carcass. The smell of death permeated the air so heavily that we could only go to the outside with kerchiefs covering our noses and mouth in order not to vomit. Mercifully, some prisoners got dispatched to dig ditches to bury man and beast together in one final effort to clear the air.

With that immediate relief, I took an axe and started to make firewood for the coming winter. Whatever possessed me to think in those normal terms during such times I have no idea. It was an ultimate attempt of a child to hang on to some normalcy in the middle of total disaster.

Whatever it was, it was a short-lived dream that came to a sudden halt. Our turn to run had arrived the beginning of May. Mutti slipped dress after dress over our heads to save the labors of her hard work. A dumped baby carriage was ripped of the wheels to make a little cart that carried our meager belongings, some food, and some water in a military canteen left by some unfortunate soul. Mutti stuck documents, money and her wedding band in her corset before we ran on to the road to join the caravan of the doomed. Schnucki was left sitting on the couch with a dish of water and a can of sardines, watching the door close behind us.

Mutti did not tell us that she had made hasty arrangements with a soldier to shoot our pet during the week. Again I counted on everything just going to be ok in time to come, only to lose that optimistic hope as we drudged along that endless dusty road under a merciless sun that beat down on us. We peeled the dresses off like onionskins trying to get relief and movement to get on to destinations we did not know. Drudging along with our meager water supply dwindling, and everybody else guarding the little that they had, we shuffled through the dust surrounded by people with blank staring gazes. They would not even flinch or glance when someone dropped to the ground, unable to go any further. The bodies of the fallen got dragged and thrown by the wayside, so as not to create an obstacle to the moving wagons and walkers.

My fear mounted that I might be the next in the ditch, feeling my strength ebbing with every step I took. Mutti didn't look all that strong either. Ulla was the one that kept up a determined march, pulling the little makeshift handcart with our belongings. We followed a wagon that was guided by two soldiers maneuvering a team of exhausted horses between the human miseries on the road of escape from the Russian troops, who were hot on our trail. As one of the soldiers turned around in his seat to secure a canvas cover over a box behind him, he motioned for me to jump on to the back of the open wagon. I was only too happy to comply and sat there dangling my legs while Ulla and Mutti got a hold of one of the planks for a bit of support, and followed closely. Every now and then a shot would ring out, leaving another suicide on the road. Some military official or other had decided to end it all. We didn't look at the corpses anymore, because in the final analyses they all looked the same.

After hours of marching, we came to a sudden stop. No one moved forward, while up front on the road a tremendous confusion was taking place. My two soldiers on the wagon wound up screaming at each other, and I noticed that the uniform of the driver did not have the same insignia as the German that had invited me on to the wagon. He was a Ukrainian (white Russian) fighting with the Germans against the

Bolsheviks who had killed the Tsar, family and their followers. These white Russians consisted of the educated, anti-proletariat population that were hunted and sent to Siberia or killed when caught. So here he were getting screamed at by some hysterical German, yelling to get the wagon moving. The horses were rearing and pulling to and fro, not knowing where to go, while being beaten with merciless fury. The German obviously blamed the Russian, who was trying desperately to get the animals under control. He pulled a revolver and shot the Russian in the head making him slump in to the wagon behind me. I jumped off, running blindly away from this murder, firmly believing that I was next in line for a hole in the head. My legs just kept running through the soggy ditch, with screams of "the Russians are coming" echoing all around us. People abandoned everything, racing towards the woods with crazed soldiers on foot or horses running through the panicky masses, having no regard for who fell under the trampling hooves. I ran with Mutti and Ulla close behind me into the forest, crawling through the thicket for cover. Under cover, we could hear the screams of the ones that had not made it.

The Russian advance had come on horses, running down whoever got in their way, and many people died. Women got stripped and raped, with their children witnessing their mothers, grandmothers, and sisters screaming, fighting and at times dying under the brutal attacks by multiple soldiers. We saw and heard it all, and hoped that darkness somehow could save us from the horrible events that had unfolded in the open fields.

As it got darker we kept crawling deeper in to the woods, becoming fully aware of many others around us. They were also trying to find some safety spot, when suddenly strong lights blinded us, and we found ourselves rounded up by soldiers. They found our situation hilarious, laughing as they herded us out of the woods, prodding our backs with rifle butts back on to the littered road. We had gone through all that to wind up captured anyway.

The dark of night spared us the clear view of the carnage that had taken place only a few hours before. We stumbled over obstacles and cadavers of man or beast, doing our damnedest to remain upright with all the back prodding inflicted upon us. Because of the dark and the kerchiefs over the women's faces, the soldiers did not pick out new victims to rape and torture. Ulla and Mutti walked with their heads way down, while carefully keeping every hair hidden under the babushka. They walked hunched over like old women and seemed to have truly aged. I felt a hand lift my face and the soldier asked my age. I held up eight fingers and got a half of a loaf of bread, which I quickly rolled up with my skirt exposing my bloomers, but I didn't care. I got away with that eight finger sign from then on. It must have been a magic number for these Bolsheviks to invoke some sort of mercy or immunity.

We had not seen that red brick building with a wide-open area around it before, and found ourselves herded towards this looming dark house. It did not look inviting at all. However, a heavy drizzle had started and we entered gratefully to be out of the rain. The large room was empty, and the stone floors covered with heavy dust. The windows were high off the ground and had bars on them. We got pushed face down on to the floor, and were ordered by the same soldier that had given me the bread, in almost perfect German, to keep our heads down. The soldiers walked between the lines that were stretched out like human sardines, popping raised heads here and there with the rifle butt. I got about three pops trying to maneuver the piece of bread in to a safe spot under my body, till Mutti reached over and with a steel grip forced my head to stay down. Little rivulets of urine ran on the ground amongst us, much to the amusement of the soldiers who watched as we were slithering around to avoid getting soaked.

All in vain, since we did doze off and wound up wet and soiled like unattended infants. The 'wake up and get out' methods were almost as brutal as those which had gotten us into that strange place. Now we smelled to the heavens, and there was not one dry panty in the whole group. We scrambled to our feet and moved towards the doors, which were wide enough to accommodate a herd of cattle. The sunlight blinded us at first, but slowly our squinting eyes opened to the scene of a so-called courtyard. It had a water pump, ready and waiting to serve us the first water we had since God knows when.

The resultant stampede became another point of amusement to the Russians encircling that building, who were lounging on the ground, sitting on wagons or horses, and even playing harmonicas around a fire while turning a pig on a spit. Some did a little dance, celebrating and clapping hands, as they watched us fight over a spot near the waterspout. Then they waved us on in the direction we had come from the day before. Go, Go Germanskis!! And so we stumbled back on to the road, the one that told the story of the day before all too clearly. Collapsed wagons and mangled bodies of man and beast contrasted starkly with the bright sunshine that was encouraging nature to explode with new blessings, to be brought by a promising spring. Strange, I thought, a total contradiction to the ugly wide expanse of human handiwork laid out in front of our tired eyes.

We had no idea of how far we had walked the day before. There were no road signs, only hordes of Russians singing on top of supply wagons, some waving at us in a drunken stupor. They all looked so different from our soldiers - the high-buttoned shirts, bloused at the waist with a wide belt; and the pants, a bit puffed out on the side, disappeared into black short boots. Their hair was closely cropped, if not shaven, and jauntily topped by a Garrison cap with a red star. They had high cheekbones and grinned a lot, a happy happy lot these victors, all dressed in a grayish brown uniform, banishing us, God knows to where and to what.

With the urine soaked underwear, unwashed thighs rubbing relentlessly against each other; the walking became sheer torture. Each and every step made us more raw, a feeling like we had razorblades between our legs. Edging towards the stream running alongside the road, paying no mind to some floating bodies in it, we spotted a fairly empty area and walked down the embankment. We ducked our behinds into the cool water, immediately experiencing unbelievable burning that made us whistle through our teeth. We didn't know whether to get up or stay. It was one of those you're damned if you do, and damned if you don't moments.

Sitting in that cool water, we looked at the endless flow of Russians passing by. They couldn't care less about us sitting in that water. In fact, they barely glanced at us. That is except for the female soldiers, who stared straight at us, and even turned their heads after they had passed. How did we miss the women amongst the men? Was it because they also wore the uniforms and carried the same weapons? We didn't see the skirts they wore. These were the 'Flintenweiber' our soldiers had talked about. They were telling their comrades that they should always save a bullet, so if captured by these females, "It is best to shoot yourself, buddy", so as not to suffer brutalities at the hands of these avengers. Stories had it that they had lost everyone and everything to the German invasion into Russia. They were driven by revenge! Stripped of any female emotion, they looked at us with hostility and hatred, without a glimmer of mercy. Looking at them, I believed every story I had heard.

We had never seen combat females. Women in the German army served as telephone operators, secretaries and such. Actually the slang term was 'Officers' Mattresses.' So we looked at these women wondering what kind of contact, if any, we will have with them. Our march back to our town was done at nightfall. When we finally arrived, Mutti fumbled the key out of her corset, although the door was busted wide open. She held the key looking helplessly at the strewn about scraps of our miserable belongings that we had left behind. She broke down and cried, with us hanging on to her trying to make it all better, when we heard a slight rustle and soft 'mew.' Our Schnucki was coming out from underneath the slashed couch rubbing his soft head against our legs. Everything faded as we grabbed him, showering him with kisses, tears and hugs. Forgotten was the pain and misery. He was ok and so were we, I thought, as I crawled on to the bed with my beloved cat in my arms.

THEY came at dawn, pulling Mutti off the couch, shoving her out the door and on to the road to town, with us in tow and scared out of our minds. The town square was already full of women, their arms filled with dirty uniforms, socks and such. All were escorted to the fountain, where they had to start scrubbing the laundry under the watchful eyes of the soldiers.

The entire scene at the square had something unreal about it. Some carcasses had been arranged in front of the school, right underneath Herr Tauber, who had been hanged upside down. It seemed to me that his complexion was bluish, but that may have been the breaking dawn. Oh well, anyway, I was glad that he was gone out of our lives.

The soldiers rewarded the women with bread, and after I did my eight-finger bit again, I got some milk in a canteen, two eggs and a bit of butter. We rushed home, fully aware that Ulla and Mutti had gotten closely scrutinized by a couple of troops.

Word got out that 'they' will have a party, a real victory bash with vodka, a pig roast, the whole enchilada. In short, it spelled trouble for the women who had been in full view during the day. Rumor had it that their commandant did not permit any more raping, but that was kind of "iffy", since no one had seen him around.

So a couple of soldiers dragged a screaming pig out of its stall, slaughtered it right there in the square, bleeding and gutting it, while others constructed a spit over a huge fire. The word *Vodka* was familiar to us from the stories told by our soldiers in the hospitals. They had tasted that stuff in the first part of the war, while marching into Russia.

One thing was for sure. The females had to disappear. We were following the frightened women into the woods, clustered at the lower base on the surrounding hills. We, the children, gathered branches to cover the frightened women who had curled up in to the hollows of the uneven terrain. We had quickly scraped the loose soil deeper with all of us digging and clawing the ground. We were frantic to save our loved ones. After all the hectic activity, the children were left to return and make believe that all was well. We paired up in the different houses, finding some reassurance in each other's presence. We listened to the harmonicas and yells, as the soldiers shouted and danced. Meanwhile, the pig was roasting and gave off a tantalizing smell, which made our stomachs growl and mouths water. The party had begun.

We just couldn't help controlling our curiosity, and since there was no light, we figured that our peeking would not cause any damage. So we watched the open fire, the roasting pig, and the soldiers drinking out of bottles, which they flung behind them when every drop was gone. The harmonica played tunes that we had never heard before. The music ignited some dancing competitions by the soldiers. They took turns jumping onto an open spot, performing neck-breaking moves, twirling and kicking up their heels, at times seemingly suspended in mid air. They were cheered on by the onlookers, who then, one by one, got hired on to take a turn as a solo performer. Always different, wilder, and better, each evoked applauds and screams of encouragement. When done, they were ready to collapse from all the exertion. Then eagerly, they gulped big swigs out of any bottle that was offered. We watched that wild celebrating bunch, who were so filled with a lust for life, express it without any social restrictions of dos and don'ts. It was so different from our stiff upbringing, where emotions were not to be displayed, EVER! We got tired just from watching them, while controlling the urge to go down there and ask for a piece of that pig. We practically had slobber running down our chins for the want of just a morsel. But fear won out. We didn't know how they would treat us, although I had heard that they were kind to children under a certain age. I had no real idea what that safe age was. Someone had said age twelve, ergo my eight-finger sign that had functioned well and to my advantage.

Despite my hunger, I just could not get myself to go near that drunken bunch. So I crawled fully dressed under the cover with my stomach growling. In spite of the ongoing ruckus, sleep and exhaustion came mercifully as soon as my head hit the makeshift pillow.

The door downstairs was not locked, since that

71

would have been useless under the circumstances, but it got kicked open with brute force anyway. As I heard the staggering stumbles on the stone steps, I tried to melt in to the mattress and pulled the cover over my head. Seconds later, it got flung to the floor by a swaying soldier, who stared at his discovery, not quite understanding what to do with his useless find - skinny, scrawny me! He lifted me up close to his stinking breath, and let me go to drop back like a discarded rag doll. He then straddled my body, holding a rifle barrel to my head asking, "Wo Frau?"(Where is the woman)?" I was shaking violently all over, squirming to get his weight off of me and somehow run, but all I got for my trouble was a sharp hit on the side of my head, causing me to go limp and unable to think straight. He jabbed me again, infuriated, asking for the woman again and again. I was not moving anymore, too stunned by pain and fear. Even when he fell over on his side to the floor, he clutched that damned rifle like a baby. I could not move. I heard him puke, finally staggering to his feet and stumbling down the stairs, disappearing in to the rowdy crowd. Maybe the stupid bastard realized by then that he was in no shape to deal with a woman, even if he should find one. I was retching, helplessly unable to stop, with the stink of his vomit turning my stomach into painful spasms. They stopped once I got a hold of a rag that I used to cover my nose and mouth. The other girl in the room had watched in horror, hidden behind door that had been flung open.

My head was throbbing; she was crying while she wiped at the trickle of blood on the side of my face.

We were alone in the night, surrounded by drunken hordes that could do with us whatever they wanted, with no one to stop them. We felt hopelessly alone - a feeling that would stay with me through events yet to come.

As the sun came up, its soft rays shined down on the mess of broken bottles, passed out drunks, pig leftovers, entrails, bones, vomit, and burned out ashes. I just wanted to get away from there. The women filtered back, carefully passing by the obvious ugly results of the Victory party, worried about what had taken place with the children that were left behind. We all had a story to tell, some worse than others, and some not so bad. It gave me some weird comfort that I had not been the only victim of some motherless son of a bitch. How does it go? Misery loves company. That was me!

One thing became painfully clear. We did not belong in that former Czech town. The farm women eyed us with hostility and suspicion, simply because we raided the fields for whatever edible food we could pull out of the earth. When there was a surprise slaughter of a cow or pig, the soldiers did not bother with the innards; and we could come home with a lung, spleen, tongue, or brain, depending on the speed we snatched the stuff away from the others. But then, what the hell, we had to eat. Mutti somehow became quite the cook, but we learned never to look too closely before putting the food into our mouth. The widow that Ulla had lived with lost most of her animals, but always gave us some bread, an egg, or whatever she could scrounge up. Soon we faced eviction by the Russian Commandant. "Get back to Berlin where you belong!" he bellowed. So there!

We had nothing to pack or prepare, other than leaving Schnucki with the widow woman. With absolutely no idea how to get to Berlin, we joined the never ending, walking crowd of displaced folk towards another town, with people just quietly joining the muted horde of refugees. The wagons were laden with what they thought to be of value, which only attracted the roaming soldiers, who would loot this miserable caravan. Running off with silken lampshades on their heads and fur stoles around their shoulders, they smashed family heirlooms, laughing and aping the exasperated victims. One thing was for sure; they had endless fun keeping a watchful eye out for a ripe female for the nightfall.

The women tried every trick to dissuade them, cutting themselves, smearing the blood into a cloth, and faking a cough which displayed the bloodstains, making the prospective rapist believe that they had a terrible lung disease. It worked many times.

I did well with my pathetic, pale and skinny appearance. Some soldiers would just press a piece of bread into my hand, or hand over a pair of shoes just robbed off some wagon. Ulla and I did pretty well with our pity act. She would beg at a farmer's wagon up front for some food that was of course always denied, while I would steal out of the food supply box in back. The people did not share; not a crumb, not a drop. Everyone was out for only themselves. We never slept amongst them, but we would crawl off to the side into the woods, invisible to the looters. That's how we came upon some German officers, in full leather gear, with their compasses, maps, and watches. We couldn't believe our eyes. Of course, they didn't want us anywhere near them, so they gave us general directions to Berlin and the 'AMIS.' That's where they were headed. To the Americans! They vanished into the night, without us. We often wondered if they ever reached the Ami's.

The walk became more and more difficult due to lack of water and shelter. At times the towns' wells had a bloated body floating in them, making it impossible to drink the water, while amused soldiers watched gleefully at our obvious distress.

On to the next town, more people joining, thousands shuffling along not knowing where they were headed; the sick and weak landed in the ditch, while their families moved on. Dead babies were clutched at the limp empty breasts of their crazed mothers, unwilling to let the little bodies go. We had old people pass us going in the opposite direction, babbling senselessly to themselves on their way home. They had lost everything, including their sanity. We just kept walking, ready to drop for want of water. Finally we found a clean well with people fighting to get their cup or bucket filled. It was a desperate, violent situation; and yet we joined right in to get that precious drink. Ulla was the first to get a tin filled; getting her drink with me practically pulling it away from her for fear that she wouldn't leave me any. Mutti gave me such a shot in the head for my unbelievable selfish behavior towards my sister, who had always been good to me.

We found an empty stable in the dark and collapsed on the soft ground, only to realize in the breaking dawn that I had been sleeping soundly in a pile of horse crap. I certainly attracted every fly with the fumes that I gave off after the horse-crap slumber night. We had to find some source of water that I could submerge myself in, so we separated ourselves from the vast number of walkers and drifted toward a town visible near some hills and woods.

There was no brook, but there were little houses that looked inviting, with windows open and curtains fluttering in the slight breeze. We spotted a cat sitting in the sun on a window ledge, licking its paws and then gliding them over the ears, fully concentrating on the morning grooming. She glanced at us, but never interrupted her cleansing activity. We knew from Schnucki that this was a very important procedure for cats, and did not distract her. However, we choose that house to enter. The front door was open, and led into a store, with shelves of vases and various drinking glasses that twinkled in the sunrays that came through the large window. There were dishes, cups, pretty bowls and bottles, all reminding us of festive occasions long ago. But no person came to ask us to see what we wanted there. Mutti held us back and called out, but there was no answer; no one came through the door at the end of the store. We moved carefully on the polished wood floor that made a slight creaking sound under our feet. Mutti knocked, and pushed the polished brass handle to open the door to a roomy kitchen with a table set for breakfast. In fact, the coffee cups were filled, and half eaten slices of buttered bread lay on the dishes. The jelly jar was open, with a couple of flies buzzing around the sweet delicacy. The cooking stove was lit, giving off comfortable warmth, with a steaming kettle of water ready to be put to use.

Mutti called several times, and then we fanned out to look for any warm breathing body, but there was no one. They had fled like everyone else in that town. There was not a living soul anywhere. We unshackled some dogs in our search, and then went back to the house. Mutti stripped my clothing off, and I got a severe scrubbing, my skimpy dress and bloomers following into that hot water. Ulla had peeled potatoes that gave off a mouthwatering smell, and life seemed ok in the ghost town. I stood there in a towel that was someone else's, and though we were in a house that belonged to who knows who, I found that all quite normal and comforting. Ulla was brushing her hair and Mutti was busy opening a glass of preserved pears she had found in a well-stocked pantry, when suddenly I spotted the faces at the window, taking in our cozy activity.

Two grinning Russians motioned me not to scream, as they ran one by one to the front of the house, joining us in the kitchen. The two bandy legged high cheeked young guys, quite jovial in their behavior, seemed friendly. They looked at the boiling pot with potatoes, the table set with three dishes, my wet clothes, Ulla, young and pretty; my mother, blond and not too shabby looking; and me looking like a young hungry child. They nodded, took little dance steps, and didn't do a thing other than making it clear that they would leave for a moment, come back, and bring something good for us. We just nodded with frozen smiles scared out of our wits. Mutti was steaming the potatoes, portioning them out into the dishes, while the soldiers backed out of the door, happy as larks. As soon as they were out of sight, Mutti threw the wet clothing at me. They both wrapped large kerchiefs around their head, and we ran like hell out of there towards the people to continue our trek, hiding behind a wagon and keeping a watchful eye on the road. Sure enough, the two had brought buddies. "Three more for the party" Mutti whispered. That was the good 'thing' that they were bringing back for us! That little town was theirs to do whatever they wanted - a trap for desperates like us to enter and be victimized. That's why the people had left in a panic, just as we did. I mulled for miles about the potatoes not eaten and balefully looked at my sister, blaming her for the gnawing hunger I felt for some warm food. She had to brush her damned hair like Rapunzel for the Russians to see. I bitched and griped till Mutti slapped me across the mouth in utter frustration with my idiotic reasoning and inconsideration. She was getting really fed up with my behavior.

I felt a need for a bit of distance between her

slapping hands and me, and carefully picked a spot that was fairly clean. I wanted to sulk in private but yet be close enough for her to see. At the break of dawn, she was all 'mommy' again, and she looked at me and said, "Oh my God!" And I knew I was in bad shape.

I was looking at Mutti, her hands clasped over her mouth in utter disbelief, staring at me while Ulla kept repeating, "I told you not to keep smacking her on the head and in the face." My mother turned to her, exasperated, telling her forcefully that for the hundredth time, this has nothing to do with the frequent smacks and slaps administered to keep me in line. I had no idea what the problem was, since my eyelids were almost swollen shut. My face felt like a balloon, but itchy and scaly to the touch. As we joined up with the others, I noticed that they made sure to leave a free space around me. They threw me angry looks for the possible danger I posed - not one kindly Samaritan in that bunch. Even the soldiers didn't come near us; that was certainly a blessing.

Mutti was guessing that I had been bitten or stung by something poisonous, and with time it would wear off. Of course she was right, since I felt fine otherwise. The shunning had its advantages, since my freakish looks kept others at a safe distance. They cleared the area when I came for water, and no one came after us when we set ourselves up in some abandoned house. We had been on the road for almost three weeks, with no idea if we had gone in the right direction. There was a constant change of direction, with bridges blown away and a necessary rerouting of ourselves back to the various starter points. Sometimes the soldiers pointed us in the right direction. The smell of the dead bloated bodies told us that the battle had raged in these parts of German forests. We couldn't look for some scraps of food in their pockets anymore, since they were too decomposed and full of maggots. So it was back to begging, stealing and scavenging for us!

Mutti was right. I slowly came back to looking normal and with that, resumed the shoving, pushing and using elbows at the water source again. We found the freight train with empty cattle cars just sitting there with a puffing locomotive way up front taking on water. We could not believe our luck, and hoisted ourselves into one of the cars, quickly hiding in one of the corners as not to be seen by the soldier guard. We gave a deep sigh of relief when the train gave one jolt, then another, slowly moving ahead in a smooth motion, then moving forward faster as we watched the outside flowing by. What a luxury, I thought, as we sat with our backs against the dirty boards on the filthy floor that had feces and urine soaked straw covering it. Just the feeling of not having to walk, but simply sitting there was wonderful. We dozed and wondered just where this train would take us - maybe all the way to Berlin? We dared to hope, only to have these hopes dashed when the train stopped suddenly in the middle of nowhere. The soldiers were cleaning out the many unwanted passengers. We all came tumbling out, surprised, scared and disappointed. We watched the train move on, in disbelief that our short-lived good luck was over, and stared down the road to be traveled back to nowhere.

It had not rained in some time, but the clouds got darker and lightening would flash in the sky like a warning of things to come. We moved hurriedly along the dusty road looking for some shelter. With the first raindrops falling, we sheltered ourselves under a huge oak tree as the downpour started. We got soaked as if someone was holding a watering hose on us. I cried in utter despair feeling lost, hungry, wet and hopeless, abandoned by the world around me. The entire situation hit me, standing there in that rain in God knows where, like a drowned rat. I had had it!

The downpour was over as fast as it had come, and Mutti pointed to the beautiful rainbow stretching across the sky in a rhapsody of colors like a painted promise. She stroked back my wet hair, telling me that soon this will be over, and oh how I wanted to believe her. Anyhow, we had gotten cleaned up in that rain, and the clothes on our backs were drying as we walked, so that was ok. Then someone spotted the big Red Cross sign with a large table set up and lots of people milling around it. We got a hot dish of cabbage stew, and Mutti finally got directions for Berlin. We were told that there was a freight train going from Cottbus right in to the city. With luck we could catch a hop. We hurried off towards the station that in fact had a train sitting there ready to go, but the wagons were open and laden with sacks of grain. We climbed on top, and found that almost every inch was taken up by many people hanging on to the grain sacks, so as not to slide off. And then the train moved, and we were on our way. However, we were always afraid that some soldier might decide to chase us back again. The trip was dangerous with the open-air seat, but we kind of dug a groove in between the sacks, making it safer that way. I was digging a hole with my fingers from sheer nervousness, and soon felt the grain. Mutti gave me her kerchief, and we filled it with the wheat to carry with us. That became our food for the next few days. We got in to Berlin at dawn, tired and hungry but in one piece, and life seemed good again.

Entering the inner city to reach our street was a struggle through the ruins, over blown up bridges, with the lack of street signs, and seeing people digging for some of their belongings in the piles of cement and bricks that were once their homes. We only found out later that the battle of Berlin had lasted a couple of weeks, from street to street, leveling whatever the bombing raids had not destroyed. So we looked at what was left of what was once our beautiful city. We made our way to the "Tiergarten", a huge natural park that had been our playground in the summer, and in the winter when the ponds were frozen solid, our skating rink. Now the century-old majestic trees lay with their roots sticking up, and the broken, burned out tanks and trucks lay scattered as far as the eye could see. The statues with their marble benches had been destroyed or severely damaged. The ornate gazebos and small buildings were shot to hell. It was truly a battlefield that had no resemblance to the park's former splendor. We felt a deep sense of loss, knowing that we had nothing but our memories left.

We finally arrived in our street with houses missing throughout, but not the worst off. We peeked around the corner, afraid to look, to find our building still standing. We approached it like the conquering hordes, and burst through the wooden barrier that replaced the door. We surprised a couple that had made themselves a home there with what was left of our furnishings. The guy got fresh right from the start, telling Mutti to take her brats (us) and vanish, before my mother could explain that this in fact is her home. We were shocked at the nerve of that creature. His dumpy wife was contributing to his tirade by nodding vigorously with an idiotic expression on her face and making whistling sounds through the space between her front teeth, while at the same time, blinking and frantically hiding the food on the table with her broad behind. They were a strange couple and certainly not from Berlin. Mutti ran out of patience with that intruder and pushed passed him in to the kitchen. We followed and he reached out and shoved Mutti's back. She turned and caught him square in the face with her fist. She had enough after what we had gone through to get there. Ulla blocked the woman and I slithered past them in to the living room set up with our bedding and blankets. The scuffle didn't last long. They had sadly underestimated my mother and her determination to reclaim what was legally hers. However, they didn't move either, so Ulla and I had to resort to stealing and eating all the food they had stored in various places. In fact we took everything that didn't belong to us. Mutti feigned disapproval, but that didn't stop us from marauding the place. He had some Russian cigarettes that she smoked right in front of him. At the end they had to flee the place with a few things that they miraculously salvaged from us.

We took stock of what was left of our little kingdom. The piano had been riddled with bullet holes. The front yard had three Russian graves with a bomb on top of a red cone to mark the fallen soldiers. That's where Mutti's flowerbed once was. The big chestnut tree looked like giant moths had eaten it. We had no glass in the windows, but at least wooden boards, thanks to the moron and his wife. Then we found our neighbor who had lost her husband and son in Stalingrad. Loni, her daughter and my lifelong friend, was alive, but she and her mom both had been raped. The fat, pushy creep that had been the neighborhood watchdog got rightfully shot while running for shelter. Someone pointed at him and yelled "NAZI", with the result of a soldier (no one was sure whether German or Russian) shooting him dead. There was a lot of confusion, and no one cared anyhow. Yelling Nazi did away with many unpleasant neighbors.

Whatever tree was still standing had been used to hang German soldiers, each with a cardboard sign around the neck saying," I'm a deserter who refused to fight for my Fatherland." These were soldiers that went to check on their families during the battle of Berlin.

The officers that were involved in the assassination attempt on Hitler got executed in a building five minutes away from our house. The wall with the bullet holes was still standing. So we heard all the horror stories of Russian rapists getting their heads bashed in, killed by some housewife or mother who took revenge when they were not watching. Many were found years later buried in the ruins.

Mutti was grinding the grain we had from the trip in her coffee grinder to be mixed with some water, since we did not fall under the somewhat precarious feeding program that the Russians had set up. We had to establish ourselves first with the regional commandant. I was the official water fetcher. This involved standing in line (again), sometimes for hours at the neighborhood water pump, bucket in hand, making sure that no one cut in up front.

Ilse, our co-habitant, had no problem of survival. Her customers simply came in different uniforms. We heard her "yodeling" as often as under German rule. Raping was against the law now, and she became a 'foreign relationships agent' so to speak. By now I had put my "barrack latrine" education with the knowledge of rapes together, and I knew exactly what she was doing in that room next to ours.

We went in search of our family on foot, reading the different messages left on bombed out walls, and finally found an apartment in a damaged building. There we stood, sunburned from walking cross country, fairly ungroomed for the lack of soap, barefoot for the lack of shoes, and yes, full of lice. My cousin Gerda opened the rickety, pieced together door and shouted, "we don't have anything ourselves," and slammed it shut. Mutti banged on it again, and this time said, "Gerda, it's us." It became quite an emotional greeting, with tears, hugs and kisses. Uncle Rudolph, my father's brother, had survived Africa, where he was chief engineer; but he came back with a severe case of tuberculosis. They shared with us whatever little they had, but could not tell Mutti if Papa was still alive or of his whereabouts. Tante Hedwig had poured some sort of vinegar solution on our heads, wrapped tightly in a cloth. We smelled like a walking mixed salad, with the lice doing a tarantella on our heads.

I got a pair of shoes that were too large, and had to be worn like slippers with the backs bent down, but at least I didn't get cut soles anymore from walking through the rumbled streets.

It was a good visit, and we returned back home hoping that the squatters had not come back to move in again. I don't remember how many days after that we heard the rumble of tanks and trucks, and people running to the corner yelling that "the Amis are here!" Mutti was wringing her hands saying, "Oh God, here we go again!" Ulla and I wanted to go and see, but my mother held on to us with an iron grip, not knowing what these new soldiers were all about. As we knew, she could not last forever with her vigilance to stop my curiosity, and Ulla became my helper. She was not sure about going herself, having had the experience with the Russian soldiers, but she knew that I was safe to get a closer look.

I left the apartment like a thief in the night, rushing over to Loni's, encouraging her to come with me.

Frankly I didn't have the nerve to go by myself. We nonchalantly walked up to the corner and arrived as if by coincidence face to face with the 'AMI's'.

A tank smaller than the German models stood foreboding in the middle of the street, with the turret open wide to permit the soldier to sit on the rim. He had lots of buddies with him on and around, sitting there looking at us with friendly eyes. They greeted us with wide smiles and waving hands, trying to make us come closer.

We noticed the white teeth, shaven faces, and groomed appearance, with haircuts and clean uniforms. They were beautiful, and so healthy looking! Here we were, pre-teen raggedy Ann's, lice biting the backs of our necks...no shoes, torn dresses, faces that had not seen any soap in ages, forget about the teeth. No matter how we rubbed them with our fingers and sometimes even with a sand- water mixture, the result was pitiful. We felt shame in front of these good looking, clean young guys. So we stared at them defiantly not wanting to give an inch of humility. We stared so hard and unblinking, wondering just what they were chewing without ever swallowing. It was a real standoff. The GI in the opening of the turret dug in his pocket to come out with a little green packet, holding it out to us and motioning us to come and get it. Such an American way to offer a gift!

We started the 'you get it - no, you get it' act. The poor guy was standing there holding out his gift to two very confused self-conscious girls behaving stupidly. Was it false pride, or shame? Whatever it was, we didn't go up to get his offering. I always said that he is probably still standing there holding out the (we found out later) packet of gum. We went home deep in thought about these soldiers who had come across the ocean, this time without bombs, and looking just like our people in Germany before the disasters.

We went home not regretting, but willing to face the music for our forbidden adventure. Sure enough Mutti stood at the ready, hands on hips, the particular lock of hair raised, her eyes spitting fire. Her deluge was loud, and did not permit an interruption for us to utter an excuse. At least there were no slaps on the head or face, since the recent swelling on the road. So that was good, and I thanked Ulla silently for admonishing Mutti then.

My mother had run out of words, finishing with the question, "So what did you see and what do they look like?" I was practically bursting with news about these Americans, their looks and uniforms, the friendliness, and their attempts to give us a gift. "Well," she said, "they sound perfect." I gnawed at the bottom of my lip and said, "Not perfect, because they have something wrong with their mouths." They keep chewing like regurgitating cows and never swallow." We found out later from other kids that 'chewing gum,' like many other things we were not familiar with, was a very American commodity.

Our trips to see the AMIS became a daily routine. Every day was an adventure in to new discoveries. They had different habits, like smoking a cigarette and tossing almost half of it away. For us it was a windfall. We just had to follow the smokers and pounce on that still glowing butt. Soon others caught on, and soon there was a whole army of people following the GI's, who usually never walked in less than twos. It didn't take them long to start playing games, like feigning to throw that damned butt, or tossing it like a bride would, aiming her bouquet at a favorite unmarried girlfriend. They usually tried to avoid letting a man get it, giving us girls a break.

At times I had quite a bounty, having walked long distances in pursuit of the smoking butts. Mutti had secured some sort of cigarette making machine and after plucking the tobacco out of the burned soiled paper, she artfully created another cigarette with paper that was not quite up to the task. The stuff stunk to the heavens, but had a soothing effect on Mutti's ragged nerves. Food was another story. There was none. Our part of Berlin became the British sector, and those poor souls had certainly not the abundance that the Americans had. Our ten-day ration of food could have easily been consumed in one sitting.

Anyway, Berlin had been divided like a pie into four parts. We fell in to the British sector around the corner, and up the block was the American zone, down Potsdamer Strasse several blocks the Russian sector, and the French got a part that was pretty, but farther away from us. Each of the groups shared responsibility for the occupation.

The problem started with 'Four in a Jeep.' Those patrols, each soldier from the different occupation force, kept an eye out for potential trouble. The Brits and Americans didn't have a problem (they spoke the same language), but nobody knew what the hell the French or Russians were saying or what they wanted. Stuck together in that MP jeep was no party, and tempers flared more than once. Granted, the Brits were more uptight, and the French deep down knew that they really had not earned the respect as a victorious fighting force, but the Russians were always suspicious and easily insulted, especially after finding out what the 'one finger salute' meant! That was only native to the Americans. We used it freely, not knowing the meaning; nor did we have a problem embellishing our language with the famous four-letter word that the Americans used so often in the most unlikely context. They were amused at our innocence and eagerness in using the newly acquired knowledge of the American language. Isn't it always the way; that one learns the social no-no's first?

Whenever there was a meeting of the generals at headquarters, we would secure a spot near the meeting building, knowing that the long tables will be filled with goodies. Trays were carried in with donuts (we called them the round things with a hole in the middle), delicious sandwiches, and coolers with coca-colas, beer and mixed drinks. I'd stand and pray for just one edible item to land in front of my feet, but no such luck. It was always the garbage cans out back where we searched for anything left over from the greedy hands of the service personnel.

The Americans had received a little booklet named OCCUPATION (Government Issue) while in route. In it, they were told NOT to have ANY pity on the starving German children standing around, but to think about the children that died in Warsaw and the concentration camps. It was the most hateful piece of literature that I had come across, discovering it years after I was already a US citizen. Fortunately for us, the soldiers did not follow those instructions.

Every street corner had some guys in white coats standing there with what looked like a big metal cookie press. It was loaded with DDT. They would pull up the plunger, stick the canister under the dress, push down and release a big puff of white powder over ones underwear; then they did the same over the head with the end result that we all looked like Pillsbury doughboys. Stuff was in the nose, the eyes, the hair, hopefully killing whatever fleas and lice were on the body...absolutely efficient, but degrading. One could get puffed several times by taking a simple walk, but then what the hell. We all looked alike. No one worried about that poison getting into our system, slowly poisoning us along with the parasites.

It was a black day when we found out that our Schnucki had dug himself a hole, refused water and food, and died. He knew that this time Mutti would not come for him anymore. It was for me the total break with my past childhood, and broke my heart. Despite all the suffering, death, and destruction I had witnessed in my short life, losing my Schnucki was the real 'growing up' call.

School started with our class of boys and girls together, making a total of 15 students. It was so different to be in a mixed class. Our teacher was a former Major who had been a stern enforcer of the Nazi doctrine during the war. He had a false leg now, and he would walk up and down in the classroom like a water bird, lifting the wooden leg as if overcoming an obstacle on the floor. His hawkish features left an impression on me from years back, when he would scan us while we had to sing endlessly and stand at attention saluting the flag with the big swastika. Now he was our teacher! I have to say that it was confusing, but ok, they said. After all, he was DE- NAZIFIED!

It didn't take long for Ulla to bring home a very young 'Occupier' Mutti was just ready to serve our watery grain soup (minus salt or sugar) when Ulla timidly convinced the very nice looking but shy soldier to enter through the open hole covered with the leaning, big wooden board that had replaced the door. Oddly enough he was carrying an English /German dictionary and a small bible. Boy was he ever out of his element. Ulla wasn't so sure about her conquest either, especially after having looked at Mutti, who was ticked, but graciously welcoming the guest. That's the social rule we were raised with. They both looked liked birds on a perch sitting on the little settee that still had legs. Mutti ladled out the watery soup, or as I called it 'thin grey glue.' My mother, embarrassed and knowing no English and totally at a loss for words, motioned him to come and eat the gruel with us. I have to say he had polite breeding, and didn't blink or cringe eating that unbelievably horrid concoction. Then the two of them sat under Mutti's watchful eye, conversing by passing the dictionary back and forth between them. I have to say that I regretted very much not to be old enough to get myself one of these cute guys in the neat uniform and the silent soft boots with a very shiny tip. Well, there was a curfew and Johnny had to leave. Ulla was not allowed to go outside, since all Germans had to be off the streets in the evenings. Good thing he left, because Ilse had obviously caught herself a client with an overnight pass. She got quite 'jubilant' over on the other side. Mutti finally banged on the wall to curb that ruckus, while Ulla and I stood there giggling our heads off. Oh, the joys of close quarters.

'Johnny' came back with a big bag full of the round things with holes in the middle – DONUTS! He also managed to explain, with the help of the diction- ary, that his mother had promised him to the PRIESTHOOD if he returned safe and sound. Did we believe it? NOOO, but on the other hand, it didn't matter since nothing serious developed anyway. He visited, was very nice, obviously lonely, and was eager to find out what these Germans were about. Coming to us was an alternative to hanging around on the streets whistling, or calling at anything that looked like a young female. It was either, "Hello fraulein, or hey blondie"! They were a lively bunch, and mothers would hurry by with their daughters in tow. However, that changed soon enough, and the troops spread themselves among the families. Boys in my class that had a big sister were like 'The CHOSEN ONES'. They had chewing gum, Hershey bars, crackers with cheese, and that weird peanut butter, which we didn't know what to do with when they shared it. It was kind of 'gaggy', and stuck to the roof of the mouth. We had never tasted anything like that.

All the while, typhus was rampant in Berlin. In order to get our measly rations, we had to get immunized with three shots, one per week in the chest, and then report with the certificate to receive our card for food. Without that it was, 'Sorry Charley, starve.' We reported to the nearest hospital and stood in line with torso exposed, only to have a medic plunge a long needle in to our upper rib area. I dreaded these shots, which were not only painful to receive, but for some the aftermath was paralyzing, and caused high fevers and a general sense of severe sickness.

I got sick right after the second shot. Mutti rolled out my mattress to the middle of the room so Ulla and she could put water soaks on my head and legs to somehow get the fever down. There was nothing else that could help, and I slipped into a delirious state. Mutti and Ulla sat by a small flickering flame of a candle stub in a barren room, with no way to help. Mutti was crying and lamenting loudly enough for a passing MP jeep to stop and take a look as to what on earth was going on there. The American came through the wood board on the window and stood surprised at the scene that confronted him there in that dimly lit room. I don't remember him, because I was drifting in and out of consciousness. Mutti told me that he immediately took the situation in hand, unpacking his first aid kit and pushing the quinine in to my mouth, and almost drowning me pouring water down my throat. Then he waited with Mutti and Ulla for the pills to bring down the fever. He explained in broken German that he had a daughter my age in the USA. He was not a young soldier. He left the remaining meds and drove off with his patrol that had come back for him.

The next morning, a package tightly wrapped in oilcloth sailed through our window, landing near my mattress. There landed some strips of bacon, and slices of unbelievable delicious white bread with pads of butter and cheese between them. For a week the packages arrived like clockwork. It seemed to us like our benefactor wrapped up whatever he could grab in the mess hall. Without explanation, the delivery stopped as suddenly as it had begun. We never knew his name.

My twelfth birthday was approaching and survival was a daily challenge. I had utilized every trick I had learned. I would jump on moving trains, throwing off wood and coal to people running alongside collecting the bounty; I would steal food out of market places, befriending someone with black-market connections, while taking some of the merchandize on the sneak. It was all in a day's work.

Then one day the extra treat fell into our kitchen. It was a bright afternoon when this very healthy, big Texan landed in front of us. He had been celebrating with a good amount of whiskey and was obviously quite hammered. He looked at us through bloodshot eyes and focused on my mother, who was terrified and yelling for him to GET OUT! while flailing her arms all over the place. He slammed a piece of paper and a C ration package on the table and babbled, "Ilse." His Ike jacket came off and with that he commenced to unlace his shiny boots, all the while smiling drunkenly and idiotically at my mother.

When he ripped off his shirt and began to unbutton his pants my mother became furious and was pushing him to the ground, throwing all his clothing on top of him. That was sobering to him, and he grabbed that piece of paper that clearly had Ilse's address on it. It just didn't mention to use the back entrance. He was soooo sorry and embarrassed, while climbing back in to his attire. We had confiscated the C ration, which he didn't notice. Mutti pushed him out of the back door huffing in disgust, till we opened the booty. What delicious things that little box held. It was unbelievable. Crackers, chocolate, instant coffee, cigarettes and matches, a small dinner, cheese, and — hurray — chewing gum, and even a tiny roll of toilet paper. What a bounty this guy brought us. Ulla and I waited for him outside to tell him that he can come ANYTIME through our front entrance to get to Ilse. So he did, always dropping a treat off for us. In essence we became the official pimps for Ilse. His name was JOE and thank God, he had a healthy sex drive. Mutti acted upset, but let's face it, she smoked the cigarettes anyway, no problem!!

The day came when she found herself a job with a printing firm that started fledgling newspaper. The boss was a black-marketeer, pinky ring and all. I didn't like him, but Mutti did. He had no wife, and she had no husband. Ulla and I watched with great suspicion, but as it happened, my school was visited by a group of British doctors, who sorted out the weakest ones of us. Since I had a severe case of malnutrition with a weight of just about fifty German pounds, I like many others, got selected to be shipped out by the 'action Stork' It all happened very quickly. We got loaded on Red Cross buses, to be put in the care of volunteer families that had to nurse us back to a normal weight. We arrived near Osnabruck in the British zone, and I was put in the care of the small town's only midwife.

Her son had just returned from a Russian prison camp with frozen feet and hands. So she had the two of us to care for. Her other son was a baker for the British garrison and lived with his wife across the hall in the big farmhouse. I had to sleep with the widow woman in the big feathery bed, so she could tend to me during the night, which was haunted by my night-mares, migraines, and inability to keep food down. I had to learn to eat every couple of hours, but the headaches were by far my biggest challenge.

The family was Catholic and very devout. They left the choice of church attendance up to me, but I did learn the prayers and Hail Mary's before and after every meal. I became fascinated with the mass and prayers. It was all in Latin and I loved it. It helped me with my recovery, and I became a repentant creature. I didn't quite know how that would work out once I returned to Berlin. After all, how could I survive without my sinful ways and talents? Anyway, while I was with the widow, I was holier than thou!

Nonetheless, during our recovery, we got put on

the scale like livestock and our weight gain was registered in a log. It took me seven month to gain 20 lbs, and hello, I had developed the first smidgen of promising breasts. I had sat with very hot permanent rollers that brought tears to my eyes, but I sported a head of blond curly hair. The woman had knitted me pretty sweaters and dressed me to the max, so with my new gained weight and hair glamour, I was ready for the return to Berlin. Well, then came the letter that sat me back on my heels.

It was a very nice morning with a lot of fog. I always enjoyed the milky veil of mist engulfing me like a warm blanket, hiding ugliness and images of surroundings, giving everything a secretive appearance only to get clearer by giving it closer scrutiny. It provided me with my own world. Even my singing remained my sound alone.

I walked leisurely in the silence of the grey mist to the town's general store that also doubled as a post office. My sister wrote faithfully, but Mutti's letters were few and far between. The smiling storeowner was only too happy to put my mail in to my hands, unaware that within minutes my world was going to crash down on me.

My mother's letter was not long, one page to be exact, and it told me that Papa had returned to Berlin and that she had decided to get a divorce. I had the choice to be with her or my father and Ulla. The tone was matter of fact, and she seemed to be cock sure that I, her favorite, would of course stay with her. As she explained, Ulla was always closer to her father. I was stunned. With one foul swoop my mother had erased the very reason for my survival and recovery. I wanted the life back that we had so long ago, the family living together as before. We all had luckily survived, and the reality seemed within reach. The pain was almost too much to bear and my usual reaction was to vomit and cry. Then the anger set in and a gut feeling to take revenge for the brutal severance of my dreams. I turned around and dictated a short telegram. "I'm staying with my father!" I sent it off without a second to spare.

It gave me a perverted pleasure to hear from Ulla that the telegram caused Mutti a great deal of heartbreak and tears. At that point she wanted to reconcile, but Papa said, "no, I have the girls."

Ulla wrote a heartwarming letter afterwards, knowing exactly how I felt. She was, quite happy that I would be returning to her and Papa, but not sure of how I would handle things. I went back to not eating, not sleeping well, or taking the days with the usual zest that I had lately developed. But by the time we got our travel orders, I had gotten a grip, and relished the idea of punishing my mother with that creep of a boyfriend. My imagination went in leaps and bounds, detailing every minute and dialog. It was just as invigorating as the news had been disastrous.

So we rolled into Berlin's collection station. Ulla and Papa were waving through the fencing, Mutti was on the other side waving with a kerchief. My heart was in my throat, but I was emotionally cold and well armed. I waved back at Mutti, while marching straight towards Papa and Ulla. The lines were drawn never to be changed again. It is an unusual thing to have a cordial distant relationship between a mother and daughter, but so it went.

Revenge takes on a life of its own. I found refuge in it and practiced it faithfully, watching coldly as my mother begged and cried. There were no more hugs, kisses, embraces. She had hurt me by trying to get a new life together for herself at our expense. Never mind that she knew about Papa's romantic encounters over the years. I felt she was a MOTHER and therefore had to live only for her children's welfare. That meant no divorce and the family stays together for the kids' sake. The outcome of that mind set also became the determination and my own promise NEVER to get a divorce when children are involved, no matter what!

People formed all kinds of relationships, not exclusively out of love, but often out of necessity. They came together because of housing shortages, business ventures, and simple loneliness. So a society that had been quite inhibited became loose and permissive. Almost everything became acceptable. New terms for living together became 'shacking up,' pregnancies became 'knocked up,' illegitimate children were 'no problem,' and whoever was in the lucky position to have an extra room and was so inclined, would gladly rent it out to a GI and his girlfriend. The landlady would be called MUTTI, enjoying real coffee beans, tea, cigarettes and other good things. That particular business was booming. The girls enjoyed all that the PX could provide: loafers, twin sets, rides in American cars, evenings in the clubs, and movies.

My school chum Fritz took me to his sister's room with the nail polish bottles all in a row on a dresser full of makeup and perfumes. I remember being particularly smitten with the Maybelline mascara in a small box that had a black stone type thing in it with a tiny brush. One needed to spit in it to mix it before applying the black stuff to the lashes. Fascinating! I was quite familiar with the spit thing, since mothers had used it as a forerunner to the 'wet and wipe' cloths of today.

So Berlin became quite the interesting place, like all other major cities. Snack bars sprang up here and there with jukeboxes playing favorite tunes, and those of us too young to be a "girlfriend" watching with envy the older girls enjoying life. Electricity was still rationed for us in the minor grids. Getting lights at two or three in the AM for a couple of hours was not unusual. It was then that I would rush to the neighborhood movie house to watch some shoot-um-up western. What a treat. Since there was no heat, we carried a heated brick and blankets to be somewhat warm on cold winter nights.

Papa had devised shoe polish tops filled with liquid paraffin and a shoelace hanging out as a wick, because we had no candles. It was ok, but as a result of this smoky stinky light substitute, we always looked like coalminers with the black soot coming even out of our nostrils. There was no work and black-marketeering became an art form. Our piano was a warehouse for cartons of Pall Malls, Phillip Morris, Chesterfields, and Lions coffee. Sugar, butter, bacon flour, dried eggs and so on were spread under beds and in closets to hide from the police. The street corners were the Malls of today, with people walking around advertising in murmured tones what goods they had on them...saccharin, coffee, butter, rolls—it was a crummy but busy crowd. All too often the police would show up to pull off a raid. So as not to get caught with the 'stuff', things went flying in to the ruins...no stuff, no charge. It didn't take us long to catch on to the general panic the police created. We would pick a corner and yell, "RAID!", and watch the stuff fly and the people flee. Then you just had to be quick to gather the windfall, and run for your life. Unfortunately word got around, and we really had to stop; not to mention move around carefully so as not to get identified. That would mean a beating. After all, we had interfered with people's livelihoods. However dishonest, most of the stuff was stolen to begin with.

One time, Papa and friends got word that the police had confiscated 100 lbs of sugar and 50 bottles of liquor. Instead of logging it in at the station, the cops hid it all in a garage - for themselves! Needless to say Papa and his companions rented a little car and pulled off a clean robbery, relieving the cops of their ill-gotten riches. It was a complete success, and all wound up in our house for the sharing.

I must say there was never a boring moment between school and grubbing. The adventures never stopped. Our problem of growing feet was another story. Papa would take a block of wood, carve a wedge, and cover it with straps of leather from his briefcase. Then the wedge got painted, and voila! a pair of stylish shoes emerged. At times the paint was still wet and I walked around with black lacquer all over my feet. The straps were too hard, and bleeding sores had to be endured, but I felt chic. This entire experience explains my closet full of shoes today.

I managed to keep my weight up somehow with the help of a food program in the school. Since the cooks in the huge kitchens were grafting the good stuff while no one watched, we got only the cabbage, minus the meat (except for the worms.) Fed up, I instigated a strike and we dumped the pots full of wormy food all over our desks. It caused an investigation into the cause of our riotous outburst, and the food improved. On Tuesdays we even got a piece of cheddar cheese and a square of chocolate. No one missed school on Tuesdays! But then, without warning, it happened. The Russians closed the borders and Berlin became an island.

The border was closed on June 24th 1948, and Berlin was now shut off from the outside world. The American train could get through to West Germany to shuttle troops and dependents back and forth. The train got stopped at the border crossing to have all passports presented to the Russian officials for inspection. There was a blackout order on the train, and taking a peek out of the windows was prohibited.

Food, medicines, fuel and coal had to be flown in to keep a couple of million people alive. So the very planes that had been flown to destroy our beloved city became now our salvation. A plane landed and took off every two minutes, and rumor had it that it was more like every minute. Many a dedicated pilot and crew lost their life in bad weather, due to stressed planes and personnel. It was a feverish activity to keep us all alive.

Life was difficult and the winter was brutal. I remember ice-skating constantly to keep warm. Then Papa presented us with Gertrude, a friend (yeah right) from olden times. She was a childless beast with only two things on her mind: sex and to get rid of us girls. She looked like a gypsy with that wild kinky black hair and black eyes. Although she was favoring me to no end, that phony, I was fully aware that she only did this lovey thing in a constant effort to get Ulla out. The bitch was really working at it! Papa was oblivious to her undercutting my sister. He just preferred not to notice. After all, Gertrud was good in bed, judging by her jubilations during the night.

But Ulla endured; it was not in her nature to fight back and stand her ground. Finally she gave up, and moved in with Mutti out of shear desperation. She was now almost seventeen years old and caught the eye of Mutti's boyfriend. It's not that he did anything other than open courtship, which in turn pissed Mutti off, and life became again unbearable for my sister. Cornered between a rock and a hard place, she rented a small room that cost her half of her paycheck just to have some sort of peace. The poor girl was working cleaning the ruins and street. It was hard labor, but gave some extra rations. In short she was on her own, a truemmerfrau (clearing the ruins). She had caught a nasty bronchial cough that stuck with her for years. Later, when antibiotics became available, it was too late. She died at age forty-four after many years of suffering.

I was always the one that got the breaks. She was always the one that didn't. Right down to the last breath, her life was a struggle, and I had not been a blessing for her. The widow that had nursed me two years back invited me to stay with her, worried that I might get sick again. The problem was that I had to cross the border illegally. Thinking back on that now makes my hair stand on end. I had to travel to the border, hook up with a stranger, pay him and trust him to cross me safely. All that at the age of fourteen! Did people disappear on those trips? Absolutely! What was my father thinking! I was hungry and that was a very strong motivation to take all kinds of chances. Six weeks of glorious food were worth it to me. For some reason I was fearless...kind of bad things only happen to others that was my way of thinking.

When I was ready to return to Berlin, the good widow had enough sense to insist on Papa coming to get me. It was a sobering experience for him to see just exactly what was involved to take that trip across the border, sneaking around through the night in unknown territory, and depending on a total stranger to guide you.

I became Gertrude's next project to be ousted, but stubbornly resisted, giving her a run for her money. She became more abusive as time went on, loosing her cool one day, and giving me a violent slap to my face. Consequently, I cornered her with a pot of boiling water, ready to dump it on her. Papa saved her just in time from my very determined assault. She declared me crazy, and did her best not to be ever alone with me again. She also stopped trying to get me out of the house. In fact she was very tame. I was finishing school and became teacher's pet by writing all kinds of short stories. When the school sent my teacher to the house offering to finance my education in journalism, Papa promptly told her that his daughter is quite pretty and will be swooped up, get married, and raise children. Yes, he was from the old school. Women were on earth to serve man. Ergo, higher education would be a total waste. My mother had done a half job on me, and my adored father followed up by destroying the other half. I graduated with excellent grades. Papa immediately signed me up for a three year apprenticeship with a beauty parlor. It's not that he had asked me, or talked it over with me first. No, it was just like that, without even knowing if that's what I wanted. Of course I didn't, and I let everyone know in no uncertain terms from day one. Touching people's dirty hair was just too damned much for my digestion. The nerve of my father to just treat me like property and make life decisions for me! I didn't understand my parents. They had been normal and good people. With the war they went nuts, seemingly taking it upon themselves to create havoc in Ulla's and my life.

The blockade got lifted May 11th 1949 while I was working in a ladies clothing store. That job I found myself. It was interesting, but though it had low pay, I could model and make extra money. Gertrud was doing fine with the little store that Papa had built her. She was running a very lucrative fish business, stashing all profits, all the while planning to get the hell out. We had no idea. Papa had met a new love on the job and didn't pay attention to very much around him. Amongst other things, he had not been aware that I was growing into a young woman. The day I turned sixteen and he slapped me playfully on my butt telling me 'happy birthday,' I turned on him, waving a bread knife in his face telling him not to ever, ever do that again! He was truly shocked, simply for not watching his tomboy "CHRISTIAN," as he called me, growing into a teenager. Soon thereafter, as we were waiting for a streetcar we heard to my utter delight and his visible dismay, a loud wolf whistle from a passing jeep, followed by a hardy "Hello Blondie!"

My childhood was finally over...and Papa's problems had just begun!